UNIVERSITY OF CAMBRIDGE DEPARTMENT OF
APPLIED ECONOMICS

OCCASIONAL PAPER 33

PRODUCTION CONDITIONS IN
INDIAN AGRICULTURE

Production conditions in Indian agriculture:

A STUDY BASED ON FARM MANAGEMENT SURVEYS

KRISHNA BHARADWAJ

CAMBRIDGE UNIVERSITY PRESS

Published by the Syndics of the Cambridge University Press
Bentley House, 200 Euston Road, London NW1 2DB
American Branch: 32 East 57th Street, New York, N.Y. 10022

Library of Congress Catalogue Card Number: 78 176251

ISBNs
0 521 08494 6 hard covers
0 521 09862 9 paperback

First published 1974

Set by E.W.C. Wilkins Ltd, London and printed in Great Britain
by Alden & Mowbray Ltd at the Alden Press, Oxford

Contents

List of Tables

Preface

This research work was conceived and a major part of it completed during 1969 when I took it up as a one-year project at the Department of Applied Economics, Cambridge. The period, the short duration of the project and the location explain, partly, the reliance on the *published* reports of the *Studies in the Economics of Farm Management,* referring to the years between 1954 and 1957, as also the rather limited perspective of this study. Much work has since been published employing the more detailed holdings-wise data and covering subsequent years. Consequently there are many overlaps. I have not discussed these later works either with a view to critically assessing them or in order to relate them to the present study as that would have meant recasting the original plan of this paper. I have, however, included references to them at the relevant places.

In planning this Occasional Paper, I was choosing between two alternatives: either, to suggest a set of mutually consistent, workable hypotheses on a number of inter-related aspects of agricultural production thereby presenting a rough but overall view based on *published* reports; or, to carry out a detailed investigation into some selected hypothesis using the more detailed unpublished information from primary schedules. I decided upon the first as possibly providing a helpful, preliminary perspective from which to branch off into more intensive studies. Although this implies that the investigation offers a necessarily tentative analysis, it appears to be a reasonable aim for an Occasional Paper. The publication of the paper, despite the time-lag and with all its limitations, rests on the hope that the effort made here to obtain an overall view of production relations in agriculture may prove a useful line of enquiry.

In the course of this work, I have benefited greatly from discussions with Ashok Rudra. I am aware that errors still remain, but without his help there would have been many more. Nirmal Chandra displayed much patience in going through the successive versions of the manuscript and offering detailed comments. I am grateful to Amiya Bagchi, Amit Bhaduri, Nikhilesh Bhattacharya, K.N. Raj, S.K. Rao, Utsa and Prabhat Patnaik and Sunanda Sen for useful suggestions. Joan Robinson, John Eatwell and Geoffrey Harcourt read through the draft and provided helpful comments. Jo Bradley patiently edited the manuscript and suggested many stylistic improvements.

For computational assistance at Cambridge, I am much obliged to the computer section of the Department of Applied Economics. I remain especially indebted to Dr. Lucy Slater for devoting a great deal of her time to the tedious work of devising a suitable program for fitting the technical frontier (used in Appendix H). In Delhi, Vijay Kumar Gupta, Chandan Maitra and Sajal Lahiri gave valuable computational assistance. To Mrs. Lilian Silk and the secretarial staff of the Department of Applied Economics, my thanks for typing out the various versions of the manuscript, and finally, to Mr. Inder Pal Singh of the Centre for Economic Studies & Planning of the Jawaharlal Nehru University who painstakingly typed out the final version.

I am grateful to the Department of Applied Economics for having offered me the opportunity to work on this project; to Clare Hall, whose warm hospitality and congenial environment made work so much easier and more pleasant. Finally, my thanks are due to the Indian Council of Social Science Research for providing me with supplementary financial assistance towards computational work during the last stage of this work.

Krishna Bharadwaj

New Delhi
1974

1
Introduction

1.1.   It is not surprising that problems relating to agriculture have occupied a prominent place in discussions of the Indian economy. The dimensions of the sector — engaging more than three fourths of the population and contributing a little less than half of national income — compel inescapable emphasis in any analysis of the country's economic situation or programme of economic action. Issues such as the role of agriculture in economic development, the priority the sector should receive under planning, the policy instruments to be adopted to stimulate agricultural growth, etc., have remained at the centre of vigorous debates. However, most analytical discussions in the area of 'agricultural economics' have been set out, explicitly or implicitly, as extensions of the conventional economic theory in terms of competitive markets. The researcher has yielded much too easily to the temptation of treating the cultivator and his problems of resource acquisition and utilisation on the analogy of the producer of a competitive firm. Such analogies give rise to some awkward problems, for example, in handling owned inputs like family labour or owned land. Attempts to impute market prices to such inputs have resulted in the majority of cultivators showing up net losses. This has baffled the theorists and has led to such controversies as whether it is the imputation of wages to family labour or of rent to owned land that is responsible for such a result! Even when the researcher recognizes the inadequacy or irrelevance of such specific assumptions like profit-maximization or mobility of resources guided by freely fluctuating market prices, he is prone to tinkering with only those specific parts of the competitive model, keeping undisturbed the rest of the framework, rather than face the challenge at a more fundamental level of concepts, categories and the nature of economic relationships. Thus what emerges is a product of manipulating, relaxing or restricting one or more assumptions. For example, the complex nexus of socio-economic conditions that underlies the phenomenon of underutilisation of agricultural labour force (the so-called 'disguised unemployment') gets neatly and elegantly summarised into a single consequence for the theory — the perfectly elastic horizontal supply curve of labour. Another attempt to likewise partially reformulate the model of the agrarian economy treating it as a departure from the competitive framework is made by introducing imperfections (in the form of monopoly or monopsony elements) in specific markets while the other markets continue to enjoy their well-behaved competitive status.

1.2.   The analytical challenge, however, emanates importantly from the rich variety and complexity of institutional forms manifested in the conditions of

1

production in agriculture. The agrarian economy which is in the process of a gradual transformation is characterised by the co-existence and interaction of multiple modes of production. The analytical complexities which arise cannot be handled as deviations from or imperfections of a competitive economy. Even the treatment of production conditions as mere production 'activities' — each producing unit characterised as a sort of a black box turning inputs into outputs — is not merely restrictive but it positively hinders a meaningful understanding of a concrete situation. Property relations between individuals involved in production activity are an integral part of production relations as are the technical characteristics of production. These property relations are particularly complicated in semi-feudal agriculture where power is exercised through privilege as much as through markets.

1.3.   The complexity of the network of market relations that characterises such an economy becomes evident when we note some of the peculiar features of agrarian markets which violate the competitive premises. Under the competitive framework while markets are interlinked, this is so only through prices.[1] Each producer decides on the use of a resource — owned or purchased — by treating its market price as an opportunity cost. In the long run, each producer has open to him the possibility of buying or selling any particular resource in indefinite amounts at the prevailing price. Under a regime of complete mobility of resources and profit maximization, with a well-behaved technology, every resource will have, in equilibrium, the same marginal value productivity in all uses, which will equal the market price of the resource. The market does not discriminate between producers, and decisions of the participants in the market are thus linked by the purely impersonal forces of pricing. Each producer decides on the basis of relative prices and his own budgetary constraint what best to produce and how. The point to note however is that any choice made by him in one market (factor or product) does not directly influence the field of *feasible* choices open to him in any other market. (See 1.8 below for further elucidation.)

1.4.   Discussions pertaining to production decisions in Indian agriculture have mainly been within the context of such a framework. To cite some common research endeavours: production functions, popularly of the Cobb—Douglas variety, expressing output as a function of land, labour and material inputs, are fitted to cross-sectional data on holdings. Comparisons are then made between the marginal productivities of inputs derived from such fitted functions (generally valued at the geometric mean level of inputs) and the market prices of the respective inputs in order to draw out inferences about efficiency with which resources are utilised. A question commonly posed, for example, concerns the optimality of labour use which is judged on the basis of whether or not the derived marginal productivity of labour equals the market wage rate. We shall have occasion to indicate in our discussion of the characteristics of the labour market (see Chapter 3) some of the difficulties in treating the market wage rate as an opportunity cost of labour.

---

1   Such, in fact, is the exclusive reliance on price links that the effects of economic activities which cannot be captured by the usual market pricing processes are excluded from analysis by convenient assumptions such as absence of externalities etc.

Some characteristics of agrarian market relations

1.5   The competitive assumptions are violated in a fundamental way in an agrarian economy in which the *extent* of market penetration, as also the *character* of markets, is very different. We may briefly mention here some of the crucial features that differentiate the agrarian markets. The point to note is that while markets have penetrated into the rural economy in a deep and significant manner, the extent and *type* of involvement in markets of the different sections of the peasantry are not at all uniform. The character of markets reflects and to a significant extent is determined by the local patterns of power. At the same time, the functioning of the markets is itself such as to reinforce the pattern of power. The situation may broadly be sketched as follows: the initial resource position defines the 'bargaining' position[2] of the participants in the various markets. The relative 'bargaining strength' (reinforced by forces of tradition, custom, social mores) determines the access to resources, the terms on which they can be obtained and the fields of feasible choices open to the individual producer in the various markets or, in short, his current production activities and his income and asset position resulting therefrom. This, in turn, influences his relative 'bargaining' position in the succeeding period.

1.6.   We may distinguish, broadly speaking, three types of market involvements that may emerge, depending upon the economic position of the participant. There is, first, the category of operators with a clearly dominant 'bargaining' position like the big landlord in the land (lease) market or the money lender in the credit market. These operators are powerful enough to be able to exploit the market from a position of vantage and, more importantly, are able to shape the character of the market relations themselves through contracts which interlock markets. (see below 1.8). Secondly, we can envisage the category of the economically very weak sections of the peasantry, landless agricultural labourers, very small owners or tenants, all of whom have an extremely weak 'bargaining' position in the markets. Yet they cannot avoid involving themselves in market operations. As they do not have enough land to cultivate, they have to depend upon hiring out their labour and hence submit to the vagaries of the labour market. Given the uncertainty of employment they often prefer to lease in a tiny plot of land even on extremely onerous conditions. (see Chapter 3). Not having enough circulating capital to produce even their subsistence they have to rely on credit, thus depending precariously upon the credit market. The higher degree of monetisation of inputs and outputs on very small farms indicates this element of compulsive involvement in markets, reflecting conditions of distress. (see Chapter 7). The third category of peasants falls somewhere between these two; while not powerful enough to exploit markets like the large operators, they can be somewhat more self-reliant than the landless or very small farmers and

2   The word 'bargaining' here may be somewhat misleading in that there may not be actual bargaining taking place on the market between individuals or groups of individuals. In part, custom, tradition, social mores crystalize the relative strength of different classes of the peasantry. To a certain extent the laws of the state (concerning, say, minimum wage or tenurial contracts) may influence the terms on the market. But these in turn may themselves reflect the relative economic power of the different classes of peasantry as also the class composition of the state.

may be able to protect themselves from markets if they turn unfavourable. They have (or can make provision for) adequate circulating capital, possess bullocks and implements of their own with some holding capacity over market supplies of output.

1.7.   The economic status of the cultivating households influences the degree of land utilisation, the cropping pattern, the level of employment and so on. For example, given the nature of the labour market, we indicate (in Chapter 3) why employment on and off farm may not be treated as independent of each other and how this, in turn, affects both land utilisation (intensity of cultivation as well as the cropping pattern) and the level of employment. We also discuss (in Chapter 7) how the dependence on the purchase of circulating capital and hence the need for cash resources may influence the cropping pattern on very small holdings. We also hint (in Chapter 5) that, given the superior bargaining position of the big landlord, he may choose to parcel out land — especially when irrigated — to the very small tenants, who in turn, will be compelled by economic necessity to cultivate their small plots intensively, applying owned inputs (particularly labour) far beyond the point of maximum net return. The landlord by so parcelling out land may be in a position to extract a maximum return.

1.8   It may be argued that the differential bargaining positions of the participants in any particular market may be fitted into the conventional models of monopoly or monopsony. What does complicate the analysis, however, is the fact that markets become interlocked through price and non-price links, given that market and social power is vested in the dominant rural classes and that the dominant party often combines multiple functions, thus enjoying a superior position simultaneously in a number of markets. When a landlord combines the functions of a lessor and a merchant, the terms of the lease are not only themselves quite stringent (given his position vis-à-vis the tenants in the lease market) but quite often include stipulations as to what crops the tenant ought to grow and the mode as well as terms of payment of rent. For instance, he can dictate the rent to be paid in kind and the time of payment. Thus the tenant's involvement in the lease market restricts his freedom to exercise choice in production (in terms of crops to be grown) and in the output market (to whom and when to sell the produce). If the landlord also possesses land under personal cultivation it is not unusual for him to extract underpaid or unpaid services from the tenant (or his dependents) on his own land. Similarly a moneylender-cum-merchant may extract a very high own rate of interest by giving commodity loans and stipulating suitable conditions on time and terms of repayment in kind. Again the weaker position of the borrower imposes limitations on the opportunities to phase his sales of output over time. Such interlocking of markets increases the exploitative power of the stronger sections because, while there could be limits to exploitation in any one market — due to traditions or conventions — or due to economic factors, the interpenetration of markets allows them to disperse exploitation over the different markets and to phase out exploitation over time as well. Thus there may be a traditional or conventional limit beyond which a landlord cannot exploit his monopoly position in land market in terms of the share of output owing to him under a crop-sharing system. Also, he may possibly fear that if the tenant is left with too small a share at any time, he may not put in as much of his own

4

(labour or other) inputs as he would under slightly more favourable conditions. If the landlord also enjoys monopoly advantages as a moneylender or a merchant, he could then so work out the conditions of tenure that he secures gains from exploiting the tenant in the conjoint markets. Thus the ability of the combined functionary to exploit in interlocked markets is more than what he could achieve operating in any one individual market.

1.9   Furthermore, we cannot presume that all the operators are profit-maximizers irrespective of their economic status. In fact we may not even presume that there are objectives of production defined *a priori* and uniformly applicable to all producers. The objectives of production themselves depend upon the economic status of the operator and different operators may presumably maximize (if maximization is a universally applicable behavioural premise at all) profits or gross output, or 'farm business income' (i.e. gross revenue net of actually paid out cost); some may be governed by the need to raise mainly subsistence foods. We have noted in Chapter 7, for example, that the very small operators who live in almost perpetual indebtedness may choose to raise as much gross value of output as possible per acre, even at the cost of having to incur debts to provide circulating capital; they may operate land intensively even to a point where the additional input costs are more than the value of additional output (see Chapter 7). On the other hand, the big cultivators, while aiming to produce a surplus, may yet prefer not to cultivate the land intensively for a number of reasons including the existence of opportunities for making profits or for wielding social power through non-farming activities.

1.10   These are only illustrative examples to indicate that, to be meaningful, an analysis of an agrarian economy would have to be conducted within this wider con-text of market and non-market relations with the peculiar interlocking of markets. It is misleading when talking about individual operators, to hypothesise that each producer confronts technical data and market prices in an impersonal environment and all are equally free to take decisions in all markets. Nor is it possible to analyse the producer's behaviour in any one single market without knowing how the markets are interlinked by price and non-price relations for the fields of *feasible* choices in the different markets are not, as assumed under competition, definable *a priori* independently of each other. Detailed information in a historical, specific context about the agrarian economy under study would be required to describe the particular characteristics of its markets, the nature and extent of the involvement of the different sections of its peasantry and the implications thereof.

The factual basis and the aim of this paper

1.11.   With growing empirical investigations into agriculture, more detailed obser-vations on its various aspects are becoming available for the research scholar to interpret in the light of his theory and, more importantly, to use to examine the validity and relevance of his theories and models when applied to specific situations. Many contro-versial ideas and concepts that have preoccupied development theorists like 'surplus labour', 'production and resource allocational efficiencies', are being confronted with specific observations. The data base is as yet neither sturdy nor comprehensive, partly because of the difficulties of organising and financing data collection on a vast scale. This apart, however, there are problems connected with the nature of data themselves. As is to be expected, the form in which data are collected and presented as well as the variables on which data collection is focussed cannot be viewed as neutral to the theoretical predilections of these who provide the data nor of those who use them. Given the issues on which agro-economists have been particularly engaged, the enquiries – as is illustrated by the Farm Management Surveys studies here – have concentrated chiefly on the question of technological input-output relations in agriculture. Partly due to the nature of data, their coverage, emphasis and presentation, the question which attracted by far the most intense discussion following the publication of the *Studies on the Economics of Farm Management* was the relation between farm size and productivity (namely, the alleged inverse statistical relation between yield per acre and size of holding). No doubt the question was deemed important for policy formulation, the planners emphasizing the problem of increasing output more than any other aspect of agriculture. This issue has considerable political implications as well.[3] Another area of research that received stimulus was the question of efficiency of resource allocation in agriculture, efficiency being defined in terms of factor rewards equating their respective marginal value products.

1.12.   The purpose of this occasional paper is much less ambitious than the preceding discussion may suggest. In fact, the allusion to wider issues is included partly to forewarn readers against the very limitations of this paper which is only a small step in the construction of a broader analytical framework. The limitation of the scope and of analysis primarily inheres in the empirical material it employs. We have employed here, for reasons indicated in the preface, the empirical information available in the published *Studies in the Economics of Farm Management* (henceforth referred to as FMS) carried out in two selected districts in each of the six states, Bombay, Madhya Pradesh (both presently in Maharashtra), Punjab, West Bengal, Madras and Uttar Pradesh, during the period 1954 to 1957. As mentioned already these studies emphasise the technological input-output relations and this bias, together with rather scanty information on other aspects of production, especially on property relations and on incomes originating from activities other than crop production and animal husbandry, impose severe limitations on carrying out a comprehensive and more meaningful analysis in terms of market characteristics and market involvements of different groups of peasantry. In the meantime considerable literature concerning utilisation of specific inputs, their productive efficiency and such other problems has accumulated. Bearing this in mind, what we have attempted in this Occasional Paper is the following – although fully conscious of the limitations of treating questions such as utilisation and productivity of individual inputs or of

3 Incidentally, the relative efficiency of small peasant farms vis-à-vis the large farms was hotly debated in Marxist works on the eve of the Russian Revolution when K. Kautsky's 'The Agrarian Question' became a focal point of controversy. See Lenin V.I. 'The Agrarian Question' (*Collected Works*; Vol. 5, Moscow, 1964) and also his *The Development of Capitalism in Russia* (Moscow, 1964). A systematic and detailed analysis of the problem was carried out by Chayanov (1966), whose approach and arguments have been revived in the current Indian context. The inverse relation between productivity and farm size is discussed also by Buck (1938), Georgescu-Roegen (1960) and Warriner (1939).

considering particular markets in isolation, we have taken this oft-beaten, conventional route. The aim in doing so is two-fold: firstly, to see how far some of the hypotheses currently advanced in the literature are borne out by reference to the empirical data and to indicate the difficulties, if any, at a conceptual or interpretational level that may arise in applying certain of the basic premises that are explicit or implicit in such formulations; secondly, to bring out how the observations concerning these partial facets of the overall picture, are not inconsistent with (or could be employed as the building blocks for) a more comprehensive view in terms of the unequal and diverse nature of market involvement of the different groups of cultivators arising from their position in the nexus of the agrarian economic power structure. Thus we have first investigated patterns of specific input utilisation and of productivity (land, labour, bullock labour, irrigation), more particularly in relation to the size of holding. (We have also, in Appendix H, discussed the question of the technical frontier in terms of multiple inputs). These are seemingly purely technological relations. The focus, given the nature of the FMS data, is on the farm size and productivity relations. After a close look at the debate concerning holding-size and land productivity, we conclude that the intensity of cultivation and the cropping pattern are the two most important factors explaining the tendency of the value productivity per acre to decline with an increase in farm size. These are not new results. However, in the course of our argument we indicate how the specific resource availability, the characteristics of the labour market affecting labour utilisation (a significant factor in explaining intensity of cultivation) and the interlocked nature of markets constraining the area of feasible choices may be influencing decisions concerning intensity of cultivation and the cropping pattern themselves. Within the limitations of the data, we have also attempted a rather broad and only a suggestive discussion of irrigation and of tenurial conditions as affecting production.

1.13.   Thus this paper touches upon a number of issues covered by the FMS. The treatment is neither exhaustive nor in depth. Each issue considered here (especially with regard to effects of tenurial conditions and character of markets) needs to be studied intensively in every region and extensively over periods and regions. In fact, a comprehensive understanding of the rural market nexus would necessarily call for a detailed historical specific enquiry of particular regions, for there is bound to be a great deal of diversity. Our purpose here is mainly to throw up some plausible hypotheses rather than to evaluate them or investigate them in depth. The findings need necessarily to be viewed bearing in mind the conceptual as well as the statistical limitations of the information contained in the published FMS reports. A brief discussion on the same follows.

FMS: Sampling design and coverage

1.14   The FMS adopted in their survey a multi-stage stratified random sampling procedure with villages as the primary unit and the holding as the ultimate unit. Two alternative methods of investigation were adopted called the 'Cost Accounting Method' and the 'Survey Method'. In each state (or region) two contiguous districts were first selected representing the typical soil-complex of the region. Each district was subdivided into two fairly homogeneous zones on the basis of agricultural and climatic

7

conditions and the villages were then selected at random with probability proportional
to the cultivating population. The ultimate unit of the enquiry was the 'operational
holding' comprising all the land cultivated by the selected farmer irrespective of
location or ownership. The selection of holding was arrived at after ranking the
holdings in each village in ascending (or descending) order according to their size.
The total number of holdings was then divided into five size groups, each containing
an equal number. From each such group, holdings were selected with equal prob-.
ability, two under the cost accounting method and four under the survey method.
Thus for each region, 200 holdings were selected under the 'Cost Accounting Method'
and 400 holdings under the 'Survey Method'. Information was collected on the basis
of two schedules, 'village forms' and 'holding forms'. The former provided general
information concerning the village area, population, livestock, soil-types, climatic
conditions, land utilisation, demographic characteristics etc. These were common
to both the 'Cost Accounting' and the 'Survey Methods'. The two methods differed
in the 'holding' forms which enquired into farm operations, costs, maintenance of
livestock, purchase and sale of products etc. Although the schedules were similar
under the two methods they covered different periods of reference. Data were
recorded intensively on a day-to-day basis during the period in the Cost Accounting
Method while in the Survey Method they referred to the entire period (usually two
to three months) intervening between the periodic visits of the investigator. The
analysis of findings by the two methods for the regions has indicated that the Cost
Accounting Method provided more reliable information. We have used the Cost
Accounting data in our study here. The reports furnish detailed data concerning
costs incurred — in cash or in kind — of production acitivities according to major
individual crops as well as total crop production. These are furnished according to
size-groups of operational holdings. Data on utilisation of family and hired labour
(in physical and money units), owned and hired bullock labour (in days and money
units), other current inputs like seeds etc., overhead charges paid in the form of land
revenue, rents, irrigation and other cesses, depreciation and interest charges on
capital, are presented individually for major crops and for total crop production by
size-groups of holdings.

Limitations of the data

1.15.   The information thus concentrates on input-output or technical relations
in agriculture, and other aspects of production receive much less emphasis. This is
reflected, first, in the rather non-discriminating, uni-dimensional, purely quantitative
information that we obtain on, say, irrigation or tenancy. For example, it is well
known that the percentage of the area of a holding which is irrigated, used as a
measure of the level of irrigation in the FMS, can be a very misleading index as the
effective irrigation depends upon the quality of irrigation — the source, regularity,
controllability as well as the quantum of water-supply. Whether an area is supplied
by well irrigation or canal irrigation crucially affects the dependability of water
supply. Again, whether it is a rain-fed or sub-soil source of supply affects the
regularity of irrigation. Similarly in the case of tenancy, the proportion of land
leased-in to land operated is taken as an index of the level of tenancy. In so far as
tenurial arrangements assume very many diverse forms in the matter of conditions

of work, permanence of tenure, sharing of inputs etc., the consequences of these variegated forms of arrangements escape our analysis. Land is, in fact, leased-in by operators at all levels and unless we take account of the terms and conditions of these lease arrangements, it would be misleading to assess the effects of differences in tenurial status on economic performance on the basis of the proportion of area leased-in alone. Our analysis of these aspects therefore carries over the stringent limitations inherent in the empirical base. Secondly, the sample, being drawn on the basis of the size of holding as an ultimate unit, may affect the analysis as the sample may not be an appropriate one for studying intensively aspects of production conditions like, say, tenurial conditions.

1.16.   A particular feature of the published FMS reports that may, to a certain extent, bias our results is that they present information as aggregated into size-groups of holdings. Such aggregation is bound to affect some results more than others. Classifying and presenting information on the basis of size-groups of holdings implicitly assumes that the characteristics of farms under study depend predominantly upon their belonging to a certain size group. To the extent that they do not, by pooling together the information about the individual holdings falling within a single size-group, the variations in their traits will be lost, as what one gets is an average figure for the group as a whole. Thus even an exceptional attribute of a single farm would be shown as if it were an average trait of the group. It is difficult to say *a priori* how far this aggregation affects our results, but wherever possible we shall indicate the particular type of bias that may arise in the case concerned. Also, since the different quantifiable characteristics of farms are presented as aggregated according to size-groups, one cannot study directly the relationship between these other characteristics (for example, say, between productivity per acre and level of irrigation) without making rather stringent assumptions regarding their intra-group variations. Hence in this paper when we do refer to such relations, they must be taken as suggested hypotheses rather than as established results.[4]

1.17   There are difficulties in measuring inputs and outputs in agriculture which are much more general and not confined to this study alone. The obvious case is that of human labour input. Given the character of agricultural operations stretching unevenly over a long period of time, and given further the possibility of stretching a single task over time, it is difficult to distinguish clearly between labour which is 'productively employed', 'unproductively employed' and 'unemployed'.[5] This imprecision enters not only into the reckonings of the investigator but even into those of the reporting agricultural worker himself. Again, valuation of assets — especially those created on the farm and for which we have no direct market valuation — poses a difficult problem. The question of evaluating their replacement value or depreciation is especially tricky when capital assets are neither of a standardized variety nor regularly maintained. In the FMS, implements, equipment

4   I am grateful to Ashok Rudra for warning me against such fallacious inferences.

5   Partly, in so far as there are non marketable, non-marketed or partially marketed material inputs, the argument could be extended to them as well. For, a dependable record of their use may not be directly obtainable. But the difficulty is somewhat less since there could be material measures of *intensity* of use in their case.

and machinery are evaluated at current 'market prices' and depreciation charged by the straight line method. Difficulties multiply when data on financial flows, rents and intterest are to be obtained. These are due not only to the absence of regular records but also to the possibility of misreporting. Unlike in industry, where the character of technology, the nature of the organisation and the prevalence of book-keeping practices possibly account for the greater reliability and accuracy of quantitative information (leaving aside deliberate tampering with information), data on the technological and financial aspects of agriculture are prone to be less accurate and to allow for much wider margins of reporting and non-reporting errors.

1.18.   Added to these difficulties is the fluctuating performance of agriculture which is sensitive to climatic variations. In this study we have covered Farm Management Surveys which were carried out over successive years (three, except in the case of Madhya Pradesh where only two years were covered), so that our results are not limited to one time point observations. The main concern here remains, however, intraregional comparisons of production relations and we have not gone into the details of intertemporal or interregional comparisons.

1.19.   It must be noted that the years under consideration, 1954—57, are prior to the emergence of the so-called 'green revolution' in India. It is likely that production relations may change significantly in their technical aspects as well as in terms of property relations. For example, the holding-size-productivity relations discussed here might alter. The new technology based on the use of improved seeds, improved techniques, on well-regulated and adequate supply of irrigation etc., even if scale-neutral might benefit the bigger operators to a greater extent. They may be in a favourable position to exploit the new opportunities with their relatively easier access to credit and perhaps also to the essential but scarce and costly inputs like hybrid seeds, fertilizers, improved techniques of irrigation. Furthermore, with investment in agriculture turning out to be a profitable enterprise, the patterns of land-leases might alter; possibly, large owners may gradually shift towards capitalist farming relying on the use of hired labour rather than parcel out their land to petty tenants. Thus if the green revolution persists and spreads, it may lead to significant qualitative (not only quantitative) changes in the village economy. Also, interregional differences may sharpen with some regions moving rapidly into capitalist production while others lag behind. The information analysed here could serve as a basis for comparison to assess at least some features of the changing conditions.

10

2
Land use and productivity

The inverse relation between yield per acre and size of holding

2.1.   Discussions following the publication of the FMS have mainly centred around questions of productive efficiency. The one proposition which attracted considerable notice and has continued to recur in discussion is the alleged inverse relationship between yield (i.e. value of output) per acre and the size of holding. Even if such an inverse relation holds, based as it is on a static, cross-sectional comparison, it does not provide a sufficient basis to judge the relative potentialities of the different size groups nor to predict the future patterns of size distribution that might emerge. Also, the comparison of productive efficiency is based on the productivity of an isolated input, land, thus treating it implicitly as the only limitational input. Despite these limitations, the 'inverse' relation acquired some significance as it could provide some rationale for arguing that the small farms were superior to large ones on 'purely economic' grounds. A double-edged conclusion, it could be employed, on the one hand, to support land reforms purporting to re-distribute land into smaller units and, on the other, as an argument against pooling of lands into larger units. Although the political implications of the finding have not always surfaced in the debates, they possibly account for the fervour the question has generated.

2.2.   The 'statistical finding' itself, however, has not had a smooth sailing and since the controversy about its validity has already acquired some history, we shall refer briefly here to the debate before moving on to our own ground. Amartya Sen initiated the debate when in his paper (1962) he stated a proposition based on the FMS that, by and large, productivity per acre decreased with the size of holding. He attempted an analytical explanation of this proposition coupled with two other observations, namely that, when the market wage is imputed to family labour many of the farms show losses, and that, by and large, profitability increases with the size of holdings. Although Sen himself expressed some caution regarding the statistical basis of the proposition concerning this inverse relation (especially in his subsequent paper of 1964), the phenomenon was taken more or less as well-established by most economists who proceeded to provide a number of alternative explanations for the 'observed' tendency.[1] Some doubts were expressed about the statistical validity of this inverse relation by A.P. Rao (1967) who, on the basis of disaggregated data relating to invidvidual holdings in five villages covered by the FMS, came up with

1   See among other, Agarwala (1962), Mazumdar (1963), Khusro (1964).

results contradicting the proposition. A. Rudra's (1968a) analysis of individual holdings in 20 villages strengthened this doubt. He noted that 18 out of the 20 villages failed to reveal any dependence of yield per acre on farm size, while in the case of one there was, in fact, a positive association between yield and size, and the remaining one revealed 'no systematic pattern'. These two studies, however, left open the possibility that the alleged inverse relationship could have arisen on account of the process of aggregation whereby data were presented as size-group averages in the FMS. The two village studies, on the other hand, used disaggregated data pertaining to individual holdings. This possibility too was questioned by Rudra's follow-up study (1968b) which investigated a number of related aspects as well. Working with size-group data, he challenged the validity of generalising the inverse relation to the whole of India.[2] Commenting on Rudra (1968), C.H.H. Rao (1968) pointed out that the disagreement could have arisen because of the use by Rudra of yield per gross cultivated area as the dependent variable instead of yield per net cultivated acre. Gross cultivated area is reckoned on the basis of actual land use and counts-in repetitive cropping on the same piece of land. (It is equivalent to net cultivated area or the size of farm multiplied by intensity of cultivation). To the extent therefore that intensity of cropping varied systematically with size (particularly if inversely), Rao argued, Rudra's formulation would be biased towards eliminating the inverse relation between size and yield per acre. Rudra (1968b), in reply, questioned the concept of size of farm (net cultivated area) as a proper measure of land input and also pointed out that the relation between size of farm and intensity of cultivation was not 'invariably' inverse as Rao supposed. Saini (1971) in a later study, using disaggregated farm management data and relating yield per acre (net) to size of holding (net area), reported that the inverse relation held systematically on the basis of a log linear functional fit in most cases (22 out of 25). A more extensive study by Bhattacharya and Saini (1972) provided some further support for the hypothesis of the inverse relation.

2.3.   We present in Appendix B our results for the aggregated data relating to the individual districts and for individual years between 1954 and 1957. In the majority of cases there appears to be an inverse relationship. However, it is not statistically significant in all cases. Although the inverse relation is not altogether unexceptionally supported, it is not yet conclusively rejected either and it may not be entirely speculative to look into explanations that have already been advanced and attempt to advance others. In fact, to draw the correct implications for purposes of analysis as well as policy formulation, it is necessary to search for factors that may explain the relatively higher value-productivity on smaller holdings as compared with the larger ones. An adequate explanation of the phenomenon would also help in assessing future possibilities — whether productivity differentials are a characteristic that could persist, making the small peasant family farms a historically viable

2   Considering farm business as a whole, Rudra reported that 15 out of the 17 results pertaining to 17 different districts showed negative scale effects of which, however, only 9 were statistically significant. Besides this, Rudra also studied in this article the relationships between yield per acre and farm size for individual crops. The results did not reveal any systematic relation in the case of individual crops. (see 2.5 below)

form and perhaps even relatively a more efficient one, or whether the relative advantage rests on a specific conjuncture, subject to change and hence of a temporary nature.

Some suggested explanations

2.4. Explanations that have been advanced so far fall into one or the other of three categories. (see Sen, 1964): (a) differences in techniques; the small holders using technically superior methods of production (b) qualitative differences in factor endowments; either land or labour on smaller farms is intrinsically of a superior quality (c) more intensive application of other co-operant inputs like labour, bullock power or irrigation. These are not mutually exclusive analytical categories. The overlap is particularly evident when one tries to identify them empirically. Thus, if 'technique' is merely identified with a vector of inputs, then the distinction between (a) and (c) vanishes, for 'more' intensive application of inputs to land is, by definition, a different technique. To avoid this we may here interpret 'technique' as associated with a particular type of productive equipment, and hence differences in techniques as different types of productive equipment in operation. Attitudinal differences (such as diligence and interest in work) between small and large farm-operators, if present, should be ultimately reflected in one or the other of these factors. Whether the difference is in matters of risk-taking or entrepreneurial ability, it should ultimately reflect itself either in the adoption or otherwise of better techniques of production or in willingness or otherwise to apply inputs intensively. Similarly quality of management would reflect itself in (a) or (c) and while these attitudinal and behavioural factors could at best be hypothesized as underlying forces the proximate factors with which productivity can be linked will be the ones recorded under (a), (b) and (c). If higher value productivity on small farms could be ascribed to superior techniques, it would be correct to assert that the small peasant households are progressive and the relevant question about the future possibilities would be whether their relative advantage would continue in the context of technological changes within any specified time horizon. If it is due to qualitatively superior inputs, the question to raise would be about the process that explains the concentration of the better quality inputs on the small farms and whether this process would be expected to continue. If, on the other hand, the explanation is to be found in greater utilisation of other inputs, the question is whether and in what sense it constitutes an efficient use of resources and what explains the unequally efficient input-combination on farms in different size-groups.

'Superior technique' hypothesis

2.5. If 'superior technique' is to be interpreted as better quality or technologically advanced inputs, the present FMS data do not favour the smaller operators on that ground. If anything 'modern' equipment, which in these years made little headway in any case, is concentrated on larger holdings (see Chapter 4). There is, however, a stronger statistical ground for questioning the 'superior technique' hypothesis. Taking the per acre yields (in physical units) of individual crops, we carried out regression exercises to test the inverse relation between yield per acre and size of holding. We have given the results in Appendix B. We note that in a majority of cases there is no significant or systematic relation between yield per acre and the

13

size of holding. In some cases[3] such a relation shows up only in parts and over some size groups, but the fact that it is not systematic should warn us against hasty generalisation on the basis of linear regressions. Moreover, in the majority of cases there is no systematic and significant relation at all. There are some cases (Punjab, particularly in the case of irrigated wheat gram and American cotton) where, in fact, we note a significant positive relation between yield per acre and size of holding. If indeed the smaller holdings were characterised by 'superior technique' it should have been reflected in a productivity advantage in the case of individual crops as well. That it is not, goes against this hypothesis.

2.6.   Our result concerning individual crops raises the problem of reconciling these results with the inverse relation which does not appear to be ruled out when the total yield in value terms is considered. The explanation may be found in the small operator's use of crop mixes and/or intensive use of land in the form of double cropping (measured by the ratio of *gross* cropped area to *net* cropped area) such that he derives a higher gross yield *per acre* on his holding. In the case of individual crops, the area actually sown is reckoned so that the intensity of cropping cannot enter into productivity comparisons. The fact that, in the case of the total *value* of crops the inverse relation weakens when productivity is measured per gross cultivated acre rather than per net acre, suggests that higher intensity of cropping on smaller farms is a contributory factor. However, as we shall see below, differences in the intensity of cultivation over farm sizes are not sufficient to explain the relationship. And the cropping pattern (a relatively greater proportion of land devoted to more lucrative crops on smaller farms) appears to be contributing to the phenomenon.

2.7.   Incidentally, with regard to individual crops, there are two possible ways of interpreting the scale of operation. Two types of scale effects could be envisaged: (i) related to the economy of the entire holding, its resources and hence to the size of holding (ii) related to the actual size of the area under each crop. The area devoted to a particular crop does not always vary positively with the size of holding. We found that there was no systematic relation between yield per acre and size of cropped area and in the few cases where there appeared to be a statistically significant relation between yield per acre and *size of holding* the relation between yield per acre and *size of cropped area* turned out to be not significant. Thus it appears more likely that the scale effect due to (i) is more significant, if anything, than the scale effect due to (ii).

Qualitative differences in land and labour

2.8.   As for the qualitative differences in lands, some evidence can be found which suggests that smaller holdings could constitute better quality land. Again, it is necessary here to differentiate conceptually between qualitative differences in land arising from differences in the quantity of other inputs applied to it and intrinsic ecological differences. The former have to be subsumed under (c), namely, intensive

3   Notably, dry bajri in Bombay, irrigated bajri in Nasik, pulses in West Bengal, irrigated and unirrigated wheat in U.P., cotton and jowar combinations in M.P.

14

application of co-operant inputs. It is indeed difficult to draw the line between the so-called endogenous soil differences and man-made differences especially since it is past investment in land which influences today's quality of soil. In any case, the effects of these two cannot be neatly separated statistically. Before we proceed to look for evidence to favour the 'superior land-quality' or 'fertility' hypothesis. we must clear up a possible objection that may be raised against it. It might appear that the 'superior-land' hypothesis should be rejected on the same ground as that on which the 'superior-technique' hypothesis was rejected; i.e. it could be argued that if the 'superior-land' hypothesis were to hold, it should show up in a systematic inverse relation between land productivity and size of holding in the case of individual crops as well. This, however, is not necessarily true. For, to the extent that the choice of individual crops depends upon ecological conditions, the farm operator would be expected to allocate his land to different crops in accordance with their relative soil needs, so that the differences in soil conditions would be reflected more prominently in the variations in cropping pattern than in the yield per acre of individual crops.

2.9.   Some evidence is available in the Bombay Report which could be an indicator of intrinsic soil differences. Land is classified by types of soil – deep, medium and light. The percentage of deep and medium soil is noticed to be higher in the case of smaller holdings and that of light soil higher on the larger holdings. Again, the proportion of the area uncultivated was higher on larger holdings. This however, should be cautiously interpreted as the uncultivated area, apart from covering uncultivable land, also includes land under fallow, under bunds, buildings and canals which may create a bias against the large holdings.[4]

2.10.   If indeed the smaller holdings are characterised by a superior quality of land, how do these quality differences come about? An *a priori* argument as to why smaller holdings could be qualitatively superior has been advanced by Amartya Sen (1964) in terms of population dynamics. Starting notionally with a situation where there are lands of equal size but of different qualities, operated by families of uniform size, Sen visualised a process by which higher per capita income on more fertile lands would induce the size of family on such lands to expand. He further assumed that this would lead to a more rapid fragmentation of such lands so that eventually better quality land would form the smaller size holdings. By the nature of the arguments involved (with their characterisation of a dynamic process) it is not possible to test these hypotheses directly. The argument has, however, certain weaknesses. First of all, it relies upon the working of the Malthusian law of higher incomes necessarily leading to larger families, and then, implicitly upon a standard

4   Land Revenue per acre has been suggested as a proxy variable for productivity of land.
    (See Khusro, 1964). However, we find no systematic inverse relation between land revenue
    and size of holding. Land revenue, in so far as it may reflect productivity of land at the time
    of assessment, which is only periodical, reflects not only intrinsic quality differences in soil
    but also the contribution to the quality of land made by other factors. Rent, another variable
    which is also suggested as a proxy for fertility differences, suffers additionally from the fact
    that rent records are incomplete and liable to a high degree of reporting errors. Rents bear
    very little relation to productivity of soil and depend as much upon the bargaining position
    of the tenant (see Land Revenue Commission for West Bengal, 1940).

level of per capita income beyond which land would be necessarily fragmented.[5]
All these are rather tenuous links in the argument. Furthermore, it does not allow
for the possibility that members of the family may seek alternative employment
opportunities or move away from the farms.

2.11.   A simpler explanation could be that since the economically viable size-
unit is smaller in the case of better quality land as compared with poorer land, it
makes possible (and perhaps encourages) subdivisions. Also, it is possible that when
the relatively small operators are forced by circumstances to resort to distress sales
to larger holders, it is the poorer quality land that is transferred, the distressed party
preferring to retain the better quality land. The latter argument is suggested by
Bhagwati and Chakravarty (1969). Also we may note that when a tenant, due to
financial stringency can afford to lease-in only a small piece of land, he may opt
for better quality land which is less open to risk of crop failure. Although land
values and rents may to a certain extent capitalise the productivity differentials,
the risk of crop failures at the bare subsistence limit could work out much higher
for the tenant than the additional cost of tenancy he has to bear. It may be noted
that in Sen's argument in terms of population dynamics the better quality of land
on smaller holdings is a result of the relative prosperity, if only initially, of the land
operators owning the better lands, while the argument here underlines the state of
relative distress of the small operators. Whether the association between better
quality of land and small size of holding is attributed to fragmentation following
initial advantage *à la* Sen or to conditions of distress, one can not infer that the
smaller farms have or will continue to have an economic advantage over the bigger
due to either of these underlying processes.

2.12.   Another hypothesis suggested by Bhagwati and Chakravarty (1964)
attributes the poorer productivity of land on larger holdings to the possibility
that they may be characterised by a higher degree of fragmentation of the plots
constituting the holding. Bigger operational holdings, they argue, may have been
built up by purchases of separate plots of land. Such fragmentation of cultivated
area scattered over distances adversely affects the productivity per acre. However,
the FMS shows that fragmentation is present in all size groups. In fact, while the
number of fragments *per holding* increases with size of holding, the number of
fragments *per acre* invariably decreases with the size of holding (see Appendix B).
More importantly, the average area per fragment increases invariably with the size
of farm. Indeed, from the point of view of effects on productivity, the size of a
fragment is a crucial variable.[6] It not only adversely affects current productive
operations (much time is wasted in traversing distances, watching of crops is

5   This, in fact, ought to put into action a tendency towards equalising incomes as Agarwala
    argues; see the exchange between Sen and Agarwala (1964 a & b).

6   To quote from the Report on West Bengal: '... fragmentation affects farms of all sizes. In
    the region as a whole, the number of fragments per farm generally increases rapidly as the
    size of the farm increases. However, if we measure the intensity of fragmentation by the
    number of fragments per acre, it is seen that intensity goes on decreasing with the increase
    in farm size. Thus farms of bigger sizes are in a more advantageous position than the smaller
    farms as the former possess bigger fragments than the latter.' (p. 29)

difficult, etc.), but it particularly hampers the creation and utilisation of assets. There are, for example, the well-known difficulties in digging irrigation channels or wells to ensure regular water supply. Sometimes attempts are made to overcome this difficulty through shared ownership of wells, but these arrangements are not always smooth and stable, and litigation and disputes are notoriously frequent. It is not possible to conclude from the data before us that fragmentation operates more adversely in regard to larger holdings.

2.13.   Part of the reason why even small operational holdings are fragmented could be that when additional land is leased-in by an operator to supplement his own, the leased-in land may not be contiguous to the land already under his culti-vation. However, not all fragmentation is involuntary. The Report on Punjab,[7] for example, observes that fragmentation continued in some villages despite efforts at consolidation, as the farm operators were interested in owning different plots of land suited to growing specific crops, say, fodder, vegetables or American cotton. Such a situation will prevail particularly when there are differences in soil varieties or if there are multiple sources of irrigation catering to different parts of the region. Fragmentation in such a case may be partly the result of diversified production.

2.14.   Another hypothesis in terms of qualitatively different inputs refers to labour. It has been argued that the small farmers, mostly working on their own farms, take greater care in performing their tasks and are better managers.[8] A rather subtle distinction has to be made here. It is possible that some crops do require more efficient and careful weeding and watering etc., and in such cases the relative dis-advantage of larger holdings in depending upon hired labour (which on the basis of this argument is not as efficient as family labour) would be reflected in the relatively smaller weightage given to such crops in their cropping pattern. If, however, these qualitative differences are not crop-oriented but general (like better management, say), they ought to be reflected in the individual crop performances as well. As we saw in 2.1 above, however, there is no such systematic inverse relation between productivity and size in the case of individual crops.

2.15.   The 'land-quality' hypothesis suggested a one-way causal explanation of the size of holding as determined by quality of land. In as much as qualitative differences in farms arise due to man-made changes this causation could be partly reversed. For example, the relatively larger availability of family labour per acre on small farms may enable them to devote labour to the creation and maintenance of irrigation facilities which, in turn, improve the quality of the soil (see Chapter 5 on irrigation). Thus the dependence between farm size and the quality of lands could run both ways: (a) better irrigated and hence better quality lands get partitioned into smaller sizes, and (b) greater availability of family labour per acre could lead to deployment of labour towards greater care and preservation of the soil. The latter, however, raises the question why larger holdings do not employ labour (by hiring as may be necessary) for the same purpose. We shall be concerning ourselves with this in the following section. (Also refer to Chapter 5 on irrigation).

7   Combined Report for Punjab, p. 10.
8   See C.H.H. Rao (1966).

Cropping pattern and intensity of land use

2.16.   It emerges from the preceding discussion that qualitative differences in inputs, so far as they exist, would be most predominantly reflected in the cropping pattern and intensive use of land. To the extent that quality of land is not a perennial attribute, the 'quality differences' hypothesis is not entirely satisfactory; one has yet to answer the question why the large operators do not undertake quality augmenting productive investments. The differences in value productivity thus finally boil down to differences in intensity of land-use and cropping pattern. Here, we note that the intensity of land use generally though not systematically or in all cases, varies inversely with the size of holdings.[16] (See Appendix B). It does in Punjab and U.P. where the percentage area irrigated is generally high for the region as a whole. The relation between intensity of cropping and size of holding is inverse although not systematic in the two districts of Bombay (Ahmednagar and Nasik). In the case of Madhya Pradesh, there is no variation over size classes worth noting — in fact double cropping is almost negligible on all farm sizes. In West Bengal and Madras intensity of cropping is higher on smaller size groups than on the larger, although the inverse tendency is not systematic. Apart from intensive land use, cropping patterns also contribute to the relative higher value productivity on smaller farms. Intensive use of land, in turn, involves the application of other inputs to land. In the following sections we shall discuss the various factors that influence the extent of application of various inputs and in Chapter 7 we shall discuss factors influencing the cropping patterns adopted by the cultivator.

3
Labour use and productivity

Varying extent of labour use

3.1.   We have noted above that intensity of cultivation and cropping pattern are, by and large, the two most significant factors explaining the observed tendency for yield per acre to decline with an increase in farm size. A higher intensity of cultivation involves more intensive application of inputs, particularly labour, to land. Here, we shall look a little more closely into the patterns of labour utilisation as well as discuss some features of the labour market relevant to questions of labour use in general and of the level of employment on different farms.

3.2.   A basic premise underlying a number of explanations [1] of a higher degree of labour use on small farms refers to the greater availability of family labour relative to land on smaller holdings. (Here labour is interpreted as workers). The FMS does suggest that while, generally, the size of family of the operator is positively related to the size of holding, the number of earners [2] *per acre* varies inversely with the size of holdings and in most cases systematically. [3] Even if the earners/land ratio differs between farm sizes, the level of labour utilisation (in man hours) may be expected to be evened out under competitive conditions due to the possibility of hiring in and out labour and of the family workers working more or less intensively on the farm. Contrary to this, however, it is noted that the small farms in fact tend to use relatively a greater amount of labour per acre. In order to see whether the latter 'observation' is supported by our data, we related total labour days per acre to the average size of holdings for total crop production as well as individual crops. [4] The results suggested that in the case of total crop production, total labour days per acre show a tendency to decline with an increase in size of holding — the inverse relation being statistically significant in most cases. With regard to individual crops, however, the relation appeared to be neither systematic nor significant. [5] Thus there

1   See, among others, Sen, A.K. (1962), Mazumdar, D. (1963), Desai, M. and Mazumdar, D. (1970), Mellor (1963), Mellor and Stevens (1965).

2   Earners are defined as 'Male members above 14 years of age working whole time on farm.'

3   See Appendix C.

4   This was done for all the six regions and for all years. The scatter, where it revealed any systematic pattern at all, suggested a log-linear functional relation. In Appendix C, we present the detailed results of tests carried out on the basis of such a relation.

5   In some cases there was a positive association between labour days per acre and size of holding but it was not statistically significant.

appears to be some reason to believe that small holdings use relatively greater amounts of labour input per acre in total crop production; but the fact that this relation is not supported consistently with regard to individual crops lends further support to our conjecture that the intensity of cropping and cropping pattern, to a large extent, explain the differences in input use over holding sizes — specifically, greater labour utilisation per acre on smaller farms may arise mainly due to multiple cropping and choice of labour absorbing crops.

3.3   To discover whether this varying degree of labour use on different sizes of holdings influences productivity of labour, we related yield [6] per labour day to the average size of holdings. Our results (see Appendix D) suggest that although there is generally a positive relation between the two, in the case of total crop production it is, in most cases, statistically not significant. With regard to individual crops except for isolated cases, no systematic relation is noticed.[7] Thus, labour productivity, although generally varying positively with the average size of holding, does not do so consistently or significantly. This positive relation is thus a much weaker proposition than the inverse relation with respect to productivity of land.

3.4   Applying the principles of efficient resource allocation in which market prices (including wage rate) reflect the opportunity cost of resources (including labour), the following question is often posed: If considerations of productive efficiency favour intensive application of labour to land, as on small holdings, why do the bigger operators not hire the labour necessary to cultivate land intensively? Alternatively, if such usage of labour is inefficient, why do smaller operators not hire out their labour (inefficiency being interpreted as a situation in which marginal returns to labour on a family farm fall short of the wage rate). One line of argument [8] is in terms of a dual farming system — the small 'peasant households' maximising gross output with the help of the available family labour (hence marginal productivity of labour approaching zero) and the bigger capitalist farms maximising profits on the basis of hired labour (with marginal productivity of labour equal to the wage rate). Such a neat division of the farming system between peasant and capitalist farming, while suggestive, is much too stylised. The link between the predominantly family-based farms and those depending on hired labour exists through the labour market. Whether one could possibly treat the wage rate as an opportunity cost for labour would depend upon a number of factors: the characteristics of the labour market, the extent to which hired labour and family labour could be considered substitutive categories and whether and to what extent decisions concerning employment (i.e. whether to work on the family farm or hire out or hire in labour) are

6   Yield was defined as gross value of output for total crop production, and in physical units in the case of individual crops.

7   We also plotted yield per labour day against total labour days to see whether yield declined with greater labour use. The scatters showed no systematic variation. (Of course, no interpretation in terms of diminishing marginal productivity could be suggested on the basis of the present cross-sectional and grouped statistics.)

8   See Sen, A.K. (1964). A related explanation is offered by Mazumdar, D. (1965) in terms of differences in marginal supply prices of the family labour and hired labour.

20

guided by the market price of labour. Given the limitations of the data basis of the FMS, we shall take a closer look into some of the characteristics of the labour market relevant to the questions raised above. We shall consider briefly such characteristics, among others, as (a) the total annual number of workdays put in by an average worker on farms of different sizes; (b) the employment of different categories of agricultural workers; (c) the seasonality of employment on and off farms.

Table 3.I *Employment (days of eight hours) per adult earner: on farm and off farm*

State/size of holding (acres)	Total employment (days of 8 hours)	On farm (days of 8 hours)	Off farm (days of 8 hours)
Punjab (1954–57)			
Below 5	207	203	4
5 – 10	227	226	1
10 – 20	263	262	1
20 – 50	286	286	0
50 & above	445	444	1
U.P. (1954–57)			
0 – 2.5	212	176	36
2.5 – 5	268	266	2
5 – 7.5	283	277	6
7.5 – 10	279	279	0
10 – 15	264	263	1
15 – 20	266	266	0
20 – 25	278	278	0
25 & above	283	283	0
West Bengal (1954–57)			
0.01 – 1.25	129	64	65
1.25 – 2.50	121	68	53
2.50 – 3.75	122	85	37
3.75 – 5.00	126	91	35
5.00 – 7.50	120	100	20
7.50 –10.00	125	104	11
10.00 –15.00	74	73	1
15 & above	126	126	0
Bombay (1955–57)			
Ahmednagar			
0 – 5	213	121	92
5 – 10	235	184	51
10 – 15	236	221	15
15 – 20	256	244	12
20 – 25	249	215	34
25 – 30	236	221	15
30 – 50	265	249	16
50 & above	228	226	2
Nasik			
0 – 5	240	135	105
5 – 10	282	262	20
10 – 15	277	250	27
15 – 20	249	222	27
20 – 25	256	231	25
25 – 30	268	235	33
30 – 50	269	265	4
50 & above	255	253	2

Total number of days employed per worker

3.5.   The FMS gives the average number of days reduced to standardized days of eight hours, worked by a permanent farm worker (in some cases, 'adult male earner') according to size groups of holdings and also by kind of work. Total employment is broadly divided into *on farm* and *off farm* (see Table 3.I), the latter consisting of labour hired out and exchanged. Taking employment *on farm*, we notice that the level of employment is generally higher in better irrigated areas like U.P. and Punjab. In the case of Punjab employment of workers *on farm* increases systematically and quite sharply with the size of holding. (The sharp increase is noticeable partly because of the wider size-class divisions — farms varying from less than 5 acres to those of 50 acres and above being divided into only 5 classes). This tendency is weaker and much less systematic in the other states: U.P., Bombay, M.P., West Bengal and Madras. In U.P. and Punjab (both better irrigated) employment off the farm is of minor significance, being noticeable only in the smallest size-class. In Madras, Bombay and West Bengal, reliance on outside employment is greater. Particularly in the case of West Bengal, the proximity to industrial areas perhaps accounts for the relatively higher proportion of off farm employment although the absolute level of employment remains low even on higher size holdings. Except in Punjab where outside employment is insignificant, employment *off farm* varies, broadly speaking, inversely with holding size, so that the inter-size disparities in total employment are narrower than those in *on farm* employment. An interesting, although not exact, pattern can be noticed in the level of employment per adult worker in regions other than Punjab. On the very small holdings where the operator has to rely mainly on employment off the farm, outside employment does not always appear to be adequate to compensate for the very low level of *on farm* employment. These operators are barely on the margin and can be considered very close to landless labourers in their economic status. In the immediately larger size-groups, total employment tends to increase, the operator working both on and off the farm, although the size of holding is still small. In the next larger size group of holdings, total employment per worker tends to fall again; it would seem that while the size of holding is not yet large enough to engage the family worker adequately on the farm (he is still hiring out labour), employment outside is not adequate to compensate either. It may be that the family worker is tied down to his farm and cannot offer himself for work when employment opportunities are available. On yet larger holdings work on the farm increases and although work outside declines, the total employment per worker is quite high.[9]

3.6.   Employment *on farm* and *off farm* cannot be treated as independent categories; the availability or otherwise of off farm work affects the rhythm and

---

9   This pattern is not altogether uniform in all regions, partly, because the size-class divisions are not the same. The sampling procedure, as we have noted in 1.14, involves dividing the holdings into five equal strata after arranging them in an ascending or descending order in every village. The size-range not being uniform over regions has led to different size-classes.

intensity of the work undertaken by the operator on his own farm through his choice of cropping pattern and crop mixes. If labour inputs in crop production are complementary over time, as appears probable, family labour will become committed to a certain rhythm of work on farm once a cropping pattern is settled upon. It may then not be possible for farm operators, even on relatively small holdings, to regulate their work on farm so as to take advantage of outside employment opportunities. Thus working on farm and hiring out may not be purely additive activities (i.e. simple alternatives to choose between at any moment of time). On the medium scale farms the family worker, while not fully engaged on the farm, may be able to take up outside work only for certain short periods. If employers prefer to hire workers who are available for a continued stretch of time or are easily accessible in time of need, such family workers may find themselves discriminated against. If it is also the case that many of the very small holdings have a single earner,[10] he may not be able to free himself in peak periods when, in fact, employment opportunities are the greatest. While some operators may thus be somewhat constrained as compared with agricultural labourers from offering themselves for outside employment, they have greater security of income from their own farms which explains at least partly why the landless crave for some piece of land to cultivate, and why, even at the cost of onerous tenurial conditions, there is so much demand for leasing-in land, even if a tiny plot. Claims on cultivation of land become all the more important as 'creditworthiness' is often linked with them; while owners of land can raise credit on the basis of land as a collateral, tenants may be able to get consumption loans against a commitment to repay the loan after harvest. Quite often the repayment is in terms of sale of commodities to the creditor on unfavourable terms. (See Chapter 6).

3.7.   It may be noted that, except for West Bengal, the level of employment as indicated by eight-hour days does not appear to be too low. Some have argued that this constitutes direct evidence for questioning the hypothesis of disguised unemployment.[11] The statistics concerning total employment even when expressed in terms of standardized days of eight hours have to be interpreted with caution, as they cover categories of work which call for very heterogeneous degrees of effort. Some operations are easily amenable to time stretching. We may expect that work on crop production is somewhat better time regulated than 'work other than crop production'. Of the latter a substantial part consists of cattle grazing and maintenance, supervisory, transport and marketing activities. In Appendix E where we comment on some aspects of employment, we consider whether the proportion of work on crop production, as also that on cattle maintenance, has any relation to the size of holding. We find that, in most cases, there is a positive association between the proportion of work on crop production and the size of holding, whereas there is a negative association between the proportion of work on cattle maintenance and the size of holding. As observed in the Bombay Report, small farmers who cannot afford to stall-feed animals or to produce fodder on their own farms, devote

10   To quote, for example, from the West Bengal Report (1954–57; p. 25): '. . . over a third of the total number of farms have just one earner, while more than half the farms in the largest size-group have only one.'

11   See, for example, M. Paglin (1965).

23

considerable time to the grazing of cattle on common grounds.[12] In the case of U.P. where cattle maintenance accounts for a fairly high proportion of labour, the small farmers are seen to devote a proportionately much larger amount of labour to this activity.[13] This arises partly because of indivisibilities; the amount of labour devoted to the care of cattle does not vary proportionately with the number of cattle kept.

3.8.   Unlike industrial operations, agricultural activities are not regulated by a mechanical, co-ordinated rhythm and they lend themselves to time-stretching, so that it is difficult to evaluate how much of the time which the worker claims to have put in is, in fact, the minimum 'technically' necessary. Such time-stretching possibly occurs more when there is not enough work around. A substantial part of labour time is devoted to marketing and transport as well as to 'social and other affairs'. These categories include rather amorphous activities. Even the permanent annual servant is shown to be engaged in 'social and other affairs' as a part of his work. If such work is treated as 'unproductive' as it is by the FMS, and with some justification, it would have to be noted that *hired* labour is put to such 'unproductive' work as a part of its customary duties.

Categories of farm workers

3.9.   To appreciate the overall employment situation, it is necessary to know a little more about categories of farm workers and the allocation of tasks among them, which are quite often determined by tradition. Farm workers are broadly divided into permanent workers and casual labour. Among the former are included family workers (male, female and children) and permanent farm servants (hired on a monthly or annual basis). Labour which can be hired out and labour which may be used on the family farm are not always coterminous categories. More significantly, they are not independent of the economic status (or sometimes even of the caste status) of the household. For example, among very small farming households women and children not only work on their own farms but offer themselves for work outside; whereas among the class of rich farmers female labour is often withdrawn altogether from crop production. In some peasant households, while women and children may be employed on family farms, they may be considered as a resource specific to the household in as much as while available on the family farm, they are not entrants into the labour market. Thus for the same size of family, labour available to the household and for hire may differ according to the status of the household. Much depends also on social conventions; whereas female labour is not such a high proportion of labour in U.P. and West Bengal it constitutes quite a high proportion in Madras and Madhya Pradesh.[14]

12   See Bombay; Combined Report (1954–57); p. 68

13   'Because the area commanded per pair of bullocks is smaller per farm on farms in lower size ranges a relatively larger share of labour days goes towards the maintenance of draught cattle on the smaller farms . . . Accordingly the variation on labour days for farm work per acre is within a range of 41–76 days but in the case of maintenance of draught cattle the range is 6–32.' (Combined Report, p. 52.)

14   See E. Boserup: *Women's Role in Economic Development* (1970).

3.10.   The distribution of work between male, female and child earners appears to follow a largely traditional allocation of tasks. That female labour is employed mostly as casual labour for certain typical operations is clear from its higher concentration in certain months when hoeing, weeding etc. are undertaken. In the Madhya Pradesh Report it is observed (on the basis of histograms) that there is a higher degree of seasonal fluctuation in female labour, male labour being more evenly distributed over the months. In the same report it is observed that this casual female worker usually does the same type of work as the family female labourer. Further, there is considerable stability for comparable months over the years in the *proportion* of female labour in total labour in spite of the fact that total annual labour input shows significant variations. In other words, there is a seasonality pattern in the extent of participation by women as reflected in the proportion of female labour to total labour in any one year. This appears to be stable over years despite the fact that the total labour input varies from year to year. Child labour is employed mostly in cattle grazing, crop watching etc. The proportion of child labour increases with the size of holding which may be due to the increasing number of draught and milch cattle. Use of child labour is markedly high in regions where stall feeding is not common and cattle are grazed on common grounds.

3.11.   Casual labour is the major part of hired labour. The permanent servant is more or less fully employed even in areas of otherwise low employment. For example, in Ahmednagar and Nasik a typical annual servant was employed for about 342 and 350 eight-hour days respectively (average for three years, 1954—57), of which 303 and 331 days were spent on crop production. (A typical male adult worker in the same region obtained productive employment for only one third of the available time, 'unproductive employment' — meaning work categorised as 'social and other affairs' etc., — for one third of the time and was unemployed for the remaining third). Employment of a permanent servant on the small farms (below 5 acres) is rather rare[15] although at least some casual labour is hired in by farms of all sizes. In the case of Punjab (see Table 3.II) where the labour input contributed by a permanent farm servant and by a permanent family (adult male) worker is given, an interesting comparison emerges. Both the family worker's and the annual servant's labour input increase with the size of holding. It is evident that even on smaller holdings a permanent servant is employed even though the family worker is not fully employed. (Reckoning on the basis of the number of standard eight-hour days, he is less fully employed than his counterpart on bigger farms.) Also the permanent servant himself is not fully employed on the same basis of reckoning on smaller farms. It is possible that the small farmers pay a lower wage to the annual servant in return for less work, or the permanent servant on small farms may be a part-time worker and may partly be hiring out his labour. In fact, the annual servant does hire out his labour, and the Combined Report (1954—57) for Punjab explicitly mentions that in some villages permanent farm servants have an understanding with their employers that they are free to take outside employment in *rabi* harvesting and threshing seasons.[16] What may appear surprising is that the small farmers employ

15 Sometimes a permanent servant may be employed when there is no adult male operator in the household. This, however, is a special circumstance.

16 Combined Report for Punjab (1954—57); p. 19.

Table 3.II   *Comparative annual input, in eight-hour days, of a family worker and a permanent farm servant* (Cost accounting method)

Average of three years

Holding size group (acres)	Annual labour put in by:	
	A family farm worker	A permanent farm servant
0–5	224	204
5–10	248	231
10–20	280	306
20–50	295	258
50 & above	389	535
Overall average	279	375

permanent servants despite the low level of their own employment which induces them to hire out their own labour. Part of the explanation may be that the semi-attached servants ensure an adequate supply of labour during peak periods when labour input is crucial and when wages for casual labour tend to be high. (In Punjab particularly, the seasonal fluctuations in wage rates are quite marked.) Also the small operator may himself want to take advantage of outside employment in busy seasons earning a higher casual wage while reducing his work load on his own farm in that period. Employment of permanent servants thus appears to minimise risks for both; the permanent farm servant is assured of some stable minimum income while the farm operator ensures adequate labour supply (or can achieve some flexibility in his own labour input) during peak periods. The latter factor would be important if small farms were also characterised by a small number of family workers.

Family and hired labour: implications for 'marginal productivity'

3.12.   Does hiring in of labour on smaller holdings necessarily imply full utilisation of family labour? As a counter-argument to the dual-labour system (family and hired) it has been pointed out that the small farmers not only hire out labour but also hire in casual labour and hence should be subject to the capitalist rules of equating marginal labour productivity to the wage rate.[17] It is necessary to understand the factors lying behind such hiring of labour. The reason may be partly technological. In harvesting periods, in order to ensure that the yield is not adversely affected, operations may have to be conducted within a very short period. This urgency to complete a certain volume of work may necessitate the hiring in of labour even on small farms particularly in the case of crops like sugar cane. There are days on which a family worker works for more than 12 hours.[18] In so far as labour is hired in to supplement family labour at such times, it does imply momentarily full employment of family labour. But no *simple* marginal productivity calculations can be applied to this because: (1) the productivity of all the pre-harvesting labour units depends upon the application of the *required amount* of labour input in the harvesting season, and

17   See, for example, Bhagwati, J. and Chakravarty, S. (1969)

18   The following table for U.P. which gives hour-wise distribution of working days, brings out this feature; similar information can be cited in the case of other regions too.

26

(2) for a similar reason, the marginal productivity of hired and of family labour cannot be treated as independent of each other; the hire of labour fulfilling a crucial need or providing specialised skills (see 3.13 below) affects the productivity of the family labour. These two features imply that the simple *diminishing marginal productivity* of labour curve employed in the traditional demonstration of the equality between wage rate and marginal product of labour cannot be postulated.

3.13.　　However, even the hypothesis that the hiring of labour is undertaken at times when family labour is fully employed is questionable. In the Madhya Pradesh Reports (1955—56 and 1956—57), where monthly distribution of labour by sources is given, there appears to be no systematic relationship between the amount of work put in by male family labour in any month and the proportion of hired labour employed (see Table 3.IV). One would expect that in the months in which the amount of farm work is less, much less casual labour (or none at all) would be employed. However, in the months of July and August, i.e., the peak season, the proportion of casual labour is around 32 per cent, while in February, a comparatively leaner month, it is 31 per cent in 1956 and 40 per cent in 1957. In the Report (1955—56; p. 38) this is explained by the fact that there are some cultivators who get most of the work of a certain type done by hired labour only. It is possible that certain types of operations require specialised skills or are traditionally done by a certain class — or even caste — of labourers. In such cases family labour and hired labour are not substitutive categories. Also on small farms where there is a deficiency of bullock power or of equipment, hire of these is often accompanied by hire of labour; e.g., carting of grains may involve not only hiring bullock carts but also paying labour charges to the driver.

3.14.　　The point to note is that neither of the two extreme hypotheses is justified: that family labour and hired labour are exclusively separable categories so that family labour is a datum for a cultivating household, or that they are substitutes so that the prevailing wage rate for hired labour measures the opportunity cost of family labour. To what extent family and hired labour can be viewed as substitutive categories depends upon a number of factors — the ruling wage rate is but one of them. The characteristics of the labour market in the agrarian economy cannot be understood without an intimate knowledge of the different nature and type of risks that various sections of the peasantry face in the labour market: their varying extent of mobility and freedom of decision-making open to them, the specialised character of agricultural operations, norms and conventions prevalent in operation-wise distribution of work and the seasonal time-patterns of agricultural activity etc. An important aspect which we are not in a position to explore adequately

18 (continued)

Table 3.III   *Hour-wise distribution of working days*

Hours of work per day	1954—55	1955—56	1956—57
Less than 8	37	43	47
8—9	43	35	25
9—10	15	15	18
10—12	4	5	8
12 & above	1	2	2

(U.P.; Report for 1954—57; p.52)

27

Table 3.IV *Sources of human labour*

Year and month	Percentage of male labour hours put by:				Percentage of female labour hours put by:		
	Family	Farm servants	Hired labourers	Labour obtained on exchange or gratis	Family	Hired (casual)	Labour obtained in exchange or gratis
1955							
June	40.0	27.4	25.8	6.8	17.8	81.6	0.6
July	33.55	28.5	34.5	3.5	8.0	91.9	0.1
August	41.5	28.1	28.5	1.9	6.2	93.6	0.1
September	44.2	26.6	28.9	0.5	10.7	89.3	—
October	36.6	22.2	40.6	0.6	11.9	88.1	—
November	50.0	20.5	28.1	1.4	19.3	80.4	0.3
December	50.2	15.8	33.0	1.0	16.9	82.8	0.3
1956							
January	43.6	18.8	35.6	2.0	17.2	82.8	0.0
February	45.9	21.5	31.4	1.2	20.2	79.8	—
March	49.7	28.2	19.7	2.4	24.4	75.6	0.0
April	57.4	39.4	3.2	—	63.6	36.4	—
May	56.7	42.5	0.8	—	82.8	17.8	—
June	35.0	21	39	5	13	86	1.0
July	38	23	34	5	9	91	—
August	43	26	30	1	8	92	—
September	43	29	27	1	11	89	—
October	37	27	34	2	16	84	—
November	53	25	21	1	13	87	—
December	41	19	39	1	15	85	—
1957							
January	36	21	42	1	46	54	—
February	33	35	40	2	30	69	—
March	27	26	44	3	20	80	—
April	31	28	36	5	31	69	—
May	36	30	29	5	12	88	—

on the basis of the published FMS reports, is the whole gamut of property relations particularly tenurial and other contractual relations, which may presumably influence production and other decisions, as also the character of labour markets. (See Chapter 8 for some comments relating to these).

Seasonality of work

3.15. We have already noted above (2.15) that the time-pattern and extent of work opportunities available to a worker off the farm and the time-pattern and extent of work he can himself offer on the labour market are not independent and that the availability or otherwise of employment, as also the degree of certainty attached to it, influences the decision of the operator regarding the intensity of cultivation and the cropping pattern. We note below certain features of farm activity relevant to the temporal distribution of work on and off the farm:

(i) The employment on the farm of a permanent farm worker is distributed unevenly over days and months so that employment in terms of standard *eight hour days* is considerably less than employment in terms of calendar days. The extent of overstatement in calendar days' employment appears to be larger in the case of smaller holdings.[19] The conversion of employment into uniform eight-hour days however ignores the fact that the actual dispersal of work over calendar days means that the worker — especially when he is the only earner on the farm — may not be dislodged from the farm without affecting farm activity.

(ii) Seasonality in agricultural operations implies a certain pattern of demand for hired labour. Work outside the farm reveals broadly the same seasonal pattern as work on the farm. If outside employment is primarily agricultural it means that given this synchronous seasonality pattern, the total level of employment is bound to be low. Secondly, seasonality also implies that the demand for labour will be more predominantly for casual hire, as continued maintenance of wage labour on a permanent basis may not be profitable.

19 The following table from the U.P. Report 1954—57 (p. 54) bears this out; while calendar days of employment are higher on the smallest holdings than on the largest, in terms of 8-hour days they are reduced to much less than a half of those on the largest holding:

Table 3.V   *Employment on crop production per worker*

Size-group (acres)	Employment in days per worker on crop production[a]	
	When all days are included	Converted into eight-hour days
0—2.5	278	57
2.5—5	322	159
5—7.5	327	154
7.5—10.0	329	181
10—15	335	186
15—20	296	165
20—25	323	170
25 & above	248	147

[a]Employment *on farm* includes, apart from crop production, other activities like cattle maintenance etc.

(iii) The lack of continuous and guaranteed employment may compel small operators to adopt a cropping pattern which, while not adequate to give them full employment, eases the seasonality factor. The following comment from the Madhya Pradesh Report is pertinent in this context. Commenting on the time pattern of employment the Report says, 'Male labour has been utilised on the farm more evenly. In no month more than eleven per cent of the total yearly hours of male labour had been utilised and in no month the labour put in was less than 5.5%. Agriculture in this region depends almost entirely on rainfall and there was practically no double cropping. Even then the cultivators had arranged their cropping pattern in such a way as to be able to spread their work load throughout the year'. (p.23) The choice of such cropping patterns in turn may give rise to peak period shortages of labour.

Some consequences for theory

3.16.   The preceding discussion indicates the limited relevance of the usual exercises of comparing agricultural wage rates with the marginal productivity of labour. For the wage rate is but one variable in the scheme of things which goes to determine labour utilisation on farms and possibly is not even the major explanatory variable. However, much of the controversy in agricultural economics has been over the question of this comparison of the wage rate with marginal productivity. One line of argument assumes that the market wage rate is higher than the marginal productivity of family labour and argues, *à la* Leibenstein,[20] on the basis of a positive association between wages and productivity, that higher wage rates are offered to hired labour to ensure higher productivity of labour. Such a casual connection is difficult to support at least from the evidence available in the FMS. While wages for certain operations are based upon the area-concept (like ploughing, harrowing, planting, weeding), others are calculated as the rate for a certain volume of work done (like threshing of grains, harvesting etc.). In periods of heavy work the permanent annual servant (whose income on a daily basis works out lower than that of the casual daily workers) is given, in addition to his regular pay, a certain amount of harvested produce or the cash equivalent of it. Thus some conventional norms of payment provide for differences in intensity of effort.[21] The Leibenstein-type phenomenon of higher wage rates being offered in anticipation of higher productivity appears to be absent.

3.17.   Another line of enquiry concerns the question whether small peasants are rational allocators of resources. This is examined by comparing the marginal productivity of resource uses, particularly labour, with the market rates of remuneration. 'Rationality' of producers is defined thus in the competitive context.[22] We have

20   Leibenstein, H. (1957).

21   That, at least in certain regions, the wage could be a subsistence minimum is sugggested by the fact that in a situation of partial or total crop failure, the share of the harvested produce given as a wage for harvesting is increased. (U.P.; Report 1954–57; p. 19).

22   See among others Hopper (1965), Saini (1968), Sahota (1968), Srivastava and Nagadevara (1972). A critique of this type of a model is available in Rudra, A. (1973).

already noted how various other factors, apart from the wage rate, affect the utilisation of family labour on peasant holdings and that one cannot treat hiring-out and self-employment as simple alternatives at any moment of time for a cultivator. The absence of a continued and certain demand for wage labour increases the hazards of relying on outside employment. This may motivate the small peasant household to plan the cropping pattern and land-use so as to utilise its own labour as intensively as possible. Given the sequentiality in agricultural operations and the patterns of labour use it generates, this may commit a certain amount of labour to the family farm so that in peak seasons there could arise a labour shortage.

3.18.   This raises the other side of the question of employment: why indeed does not wage-based large-scale farming develop? Restating the question, why do big landholders not invest in land and hire labour as capitalist farmers? The answer cannot be a simple one. Since there may be more lucrative avenues of investment, like money lending and speculation in land, they may not find productive investments in land as attractive. It has been observed in the FMS that not only do the small holdings incur losses (when all costs are inputed) but so also do a number of large holdings. The surrounding poverty and land hunger do provide a fertile ground for exploitation through usury and tenancy. Especially when crops are prone to climatic risks there are no well-developed markets for the more lucrative agricultural products, and when transport and communication links are not well developed, the rich in the agrarian economy may find exploitation through usury and tenancy much more profitable. (See below, notes on cropping pattern).[23] Further, given that the labour supply may not be regular in peak seasons and may be short, the rich peasants may want to restrict their dependence on hired labour. All in all, what may emerge is a situation in which intensively cultivated small peasant farms and less intensively cultivated large holdings mutually reinforce each other in a fairly stable pattern. We are here describing the situation which appears to have existed around 1957. We may expect that the appearance of rapid technological changes on the agrarian scene would alter the situation at least in some 'progressive' areas. It is possible that large scale farming may become increasingly attractive and the market for labour may grow with capitalist farming. On the other hand it is possible that rich peasants may resort to mechanisation while continuing to maintain the system of semi-feudal attached labour. Some evidence in this direction is available in the 'green revolution' belt of Punjab where labour has been imported from neighbouring areas of U.P. and settled as attached labour.[24] A detailed discussion of these is beyond the scope of this occasional paper.

23 It has been suggested that where the landowner combines in himself the functions of a lessor and a money-lender to his tenant, he may not be interested in allowing the productivity of land to increase beyond a point, as the economic betterment of the tenant-share-cropper would reduce his demand for consumption loans. The landlord's income from usury may thus have a trade off against his income from production. Such a situation may end up with relatively stagnant production conditions. (See Bhaduri, A. 1973).

24 See, among others, Ladejinsky, W. (1969) and Bardhan, P. (1970).

4
Other inputs: bullock labour and machinery

4.1.   Here we shall consider utilisation of inputs other than land and labour. Specifically, we shall concern ourselves with the following question: is the relatively greater use of labour on smaller holdings accompanied by lower use of other inputs? We shall also attempt to identify favourable or constraining factors, if any, operating on the use of these inputs on different size-classes of holdings.

Bullock labour: availability

4.2.   In the economy of crop production bullock labour plays an important part. In fact, the bullock is a multipurpose good for the cultivator; it is a major, if not the only, source of draught power used extensively in ploughing, harvesting, irrigation and transport operations. It is a capital asset to the cultivator, determining his social status and standing with creditors. It is a source of supply of manure to the farm and, when used in breeding, it is a reproductive capital asset. Thus it combines within itself, as K.N. Raj[1] observes, a number of functions, as a capital good producing a capital good as well as a capital good providing services. The ownership of a bullock, like the possession of a right to cultivation, is a matter of economic strength and security, apart from being a symbol of social prestige. Thus the rationale of owning bullocks cannot be judged on the basis of crop production activity alone.

4.3.   The distribution of bullocks over holdings is extremely uneven. A high proportion of the small cultivators have a single bullock or none, while a pair is the relevant unit for a number of operations. For example, in Ahmednagar district of Bombay, 20.6 per cent of total holdings were without bullocks, of which a majority — about 11.9 per cent — were holdings below 5 acres. The situation was relatively better in Nasik, the other, better-irrigated district of Bombay, with only 8.1 per cent having no bullocks at all and 1.3 per cent having just one. The fact that in both districts, holdings with two bullocks or more predominated (about 72 per cent in Ahmednagar and 82 per cent in Nasik) underlines the operational requirement of a pair for ploughing (with the use of 'mhot'). In West Bengal about 36 per cent of the farms did not possess any draught cattle and as such they depended wholly upon hired bullock labour or on that given in exchange for labour. About nine per cent

1   See K.N. Raj, (1968).

of the sample farms owned one draught animal. In U.P. where bullocks are utilised predominately in irrigation and for threshing purposes, the largest number of farms (about half) were two bullock farms, with the size groups above 10 acres usually having more than two. On 3 per cent of holdings, mostly below 2.5 acres in size, there were no bullocks and 11.4 per cent, mainly concentrated in the size range below 5 acres, had only one.

4.4.   While the number of draught cattle is thus unevenly distributed unfavourably to the smaller holdings, the number of draught cattle *per acre* shows an inverse trend with the average size of holding (see Table 4.I). Partly this is to be explained by the indivisibility of bullocks as an asset; the larger holdings are in a position to utilise bullocks more fully so that the area operated by a pair of bullocks is higher in their case. Thus the apparently higher *average* availability of bullocks per acre on smaller size-groups conceals both the disadvantages from which *individual* small holdings might suffer: either possessing no draught cattle or inadequate numbers or, while possessing them, not being able to utilise them economically. The maintenance cost of bullocks works almost like an overhead cost for the cultivator, to a certain extent independent of the services obtained. The cost is quite high and since fodder is the main part of it, the number of bullocks that a farm can maintain is partly dependent upon the possibility of providing fodder on the farm or on common ground. There is some flexibility, however. Smaller cultivators spend much less on maintaining bullocks, sometimes by keeping lower quality breeds, or by spending much less on fodder and feeds. Even then, as we saw in Chapter 3, they have to allocate a higher proportion of their labour to cattle maintenance.

4.5.   The degree of utilisation of bullocks also works unfavourably to the small farmers. Since bullocks are needed for certain specific operations in crop production, there is a high degree of seasonality in their use. Other uses of bullocks, such as for transport, are tied up with the possession of a cart and other such accessories and thus may not be within the reach of small operators. The number of days of employment of owned bullocks (Table 4.I) reveals the low degree of utilisation on small farms relative to the larger holdings. Futhermore, even on the very large holdings there is a substantial degree of unemployment of draught cattle. This incidentally relates the question of surplus cattle to the land distribution, with a predominance of small holdings, in the village economy. Given the indivisibility of draught cattle as an asset, and given the extreme seasonality in the use of their services (so that in peak seasons it is difficult to get them on hire), each holding whether small or large has to provide its own draught cattle despite the inevitable low utilisation. That this affects the smaller holdings relatively more adversely can be seen from the fact that the cost per working day is much higher for them compared with that for larger holdings. (see Table 4.I).

Utilisation of bullock labour

4.6.   We studied the pattern of bullock labour utilisation relating total bullock labour days (hired and family) per acre to average size of holding, in the case of

Table 4.I Bullock labour: availability, employment and cost (Average for 1954-57)

State/size group (acres)	No. of bullocks (per farm)		Average cultivated area per pair (acres)		Bullock labour days per acre — Family (Both districts)		Hired (Both districts)		Maintenance cost per working day (Rs)	
West Bengal[a]	H	24P	H	24P					H	24P
0.01–1.25	0.56	0.43	2.50	3.34	5.37		10.08		7.50	5.59
1.25–2.50	1.27	1.16	2.86	3.15	12.32		5.79		2.74	4.47
2.51–3.75	1.58	1.80	3.98	3.49	13.57		2.73		3.44	5.31
3.76–5.00	1.89	2.02	4.56	4.36	13.96		2.27		1.85	2.59
5.01–7.50	1.91	2.66	6.19	4.65	15.62		1.65		1.89	2.28
7.51–10.00	2.54	2.87	6.65	5.83	14.76		1.30		2.45	2.84
10.01–15.00	3.50	3.42	6.94	7.11	8.56		6.00		2.08	3.49
Above 15	5.06	5.46	8.92	6.30	12.07		0.37		1.82	3.96
Bombay[b]	A	N			A	N	A	N	A	N
Below 5	0.6	0.7			23.3	21.3	5.6	17.8	0.65	0.97
5–10	1.7	2.5			26.3	49.2	2.3	0.2	0.75	0.65
10–15	2.4	1.9			24.3	35.6	0.3	0.2	0.65	0.76
15–20	2.0	2.7			17.9	15.7	3.1	0.1	0.55	0.74
20–25	2.5	2.9			15.6	18.3	1.2	0.2	0.64	0.51
25–30	3.8	3.1			14.2	19.6	1.9	0.3	0.56	0.45
30–50	3.9	4.1			16.8	15.1	1.6	0.4	0.50	0.61
50 and above	6.1	6.9			11.7	4.4	3.2	5.1	0.47	0.64

Table 4.I (Continued)

State/size (acres)	No. of bullocks (per acre)	Average cultivated area per pair (acres)	Bullock labour days per acre		Maintenance cost per working day (Rs)
			Family	Hired	
Punjab					
0–5	0.40	5.0	18.5	–	2.1
5–10	0.27	7.4	18.4	0.1	1.8
10–20	0.20	10.3	17.5	0.2	1.9
20–50	0.13	15.6	15.2	0.1	1.8
50 and above	0.62	32.3	11.2	1.4	1.7
			Bullock labour days (per farm)		
U.P.					
Below 2.5	0.75	2.8	22	39	3.84
2.5–5.0	0.47	4.3	21	82	2.85
5.0–7.5	0.27	5.8	21	131	2.49
7.5–10.0	0.26	7.6	17	152	2.35
10–15	0.25	8.2	16	188	2.40
15–20	0.22	9.0	14	247	2.37
20–25	0.19	11.0	14	294	2.21
25 and above	0.18	11.8	13	411	2.26

a H stands for Hooghly and 24P for 24 Paraganas districts.
b A stands for Ahmednagar and N for Nasik districts.

total crop production as well as individual crops (see Appendix F). We found that in the case of total crop production there appeared to be, in most cases, an inverse relation between bullock labour days per acre and size of holding; this relation was significant for Bombay, Madras and Punjab, but was weak in the case of West Bengal and Madhya Pradesh. In the case of individual crops, however, the relation, although negative in all cases except a few, was not statistically significant. In the case of a few crops, especially the irrigated ones, there appeared to be a positive relation, with bullock labour per acre increasing with size of holding, but this did not persist over all years.

4.7.   One explanation that immediately suggests itself, as it ties in with our earlier discussion is that, given the fact that the small holdings too are under a social and economic compulsion to own bullocks and given the higher availability of bullocks *per acre*, small farmers may try to utilise them as fully as possible. However, the proportion of hired bullock labour to owned bullock labour is also high on these farms and decreases as the size of holding increases. This may be partly due to the fact that possession of a single bullock is inadequate for at least some of the operations. Therefore while the owned bullock remains unemployed in non-peak seasons, for at least part of the time that it is employed, the cultivator may have to supplement its services by hiring in another. Part of the bullock hire is for transport purposes when the cart, the bullocks and sometimes the labour too have to be paid hire charges. Of course a number of holdings in very small size-groups are totally dependent upon hired bullocks. The need to hire in bullock labour (for lack of, or inadequacy of, owned bullock power) should imply that small cultivators will attempt to economise on bullock use wherever possible particularly since the hire charges are not low. (The hiring party has to provide maintenance plus a hire cost for the period).

4.8.   We considered the question whether the use of human labour and of bullock labour are complementary as is sometimes suggested, so that the higher use of human labour on smaller farms is accompanied by higher bullock use as well. We plotted total bullock labour days (owned and hired) against total human labour days (family and hired), for total crop production as well as individual crops, for the three years of the enquiry and for each of the districts under study. In the case of total crop production, the scatter indicated points lying along a positively inclined ray suggesting near proportionality between the two for Punjab, Bombay, Madras and U.P., but not for West Bengal where the scatter appeared haphazard. With regard to individual crops no such systematic relation was observed. In a few cases the points lay around an almost horizontal line, suggesting that there was a more or less steady level of bullock labour input with varying human labour.[2]

2   For reasons mentioned in 1.16, this exercise has only suggestive value. In Appendix F, we have given the results of statistically relating the ratio of human to bullock labour and size of holding.

Table 4.II   *Value of implements per acre*

State/size (acres)	Punjab (Rs)
0–5	38
5–10	29
10–20	28
20–50	22
50 and above	12

	Bombay		M.P.
	Ahmednagar (Rs)	Nasik (Rs)	(Rs)
0–5	23	16	22.9
5–10	14	26	12.02
10–15	15	12	7.1
15–20	6	12	8.6
20–25	4	12	8.4
25–30	7	6	17.7
30–50	31	25	14.4
50 and above	3	5	17.25

	West Bengal	
	Hooghly (Rs)	24 Paraganas (Rs)
0.01–1.25	13.9	8.4
1.25–2.50	13.6	7.7
2.50–3.75	9.3	6.4
3.76–5.00	8.7	6.4
5.01–7.50	7.8	6.4
7.51–10.00	7.4	7.0
10 –15	10.2	5.4
15 and above	10.3	4.7

	U.P. (Rs)	Madras (Rs)
Below 2.5	6.10	31.4
2.5–5	6.8	27.9
5 –7.5	4.2	19.2
7.5–10	4.6	34.2
10–15	4.1	10.0
15–20	4.0	15.8
20–25	4.7	21.5
25 and above	4.0	21.3

4.9.   Thus in total crop production there appears to be some complementarity between bullock and human labour. Both are used more on smaller size-classes of holdings as compared to the larger. In the case of individual crops, no systematic relations obtain. The explanation for the relatively greater use of bullock labour may perhaps be related to the fact that the smaller holdings have a higher percentage of irrigated area, and working of irrigation as well as production of irrigated crops absorbs a relatively higher quantum of bullock labour (see chapter 5 below). The cropping pattern thus could be such as to absorb relatively more bullock labour on smaller farms. Also, the greater intensity of cultivation on the smaller holdings implies that more bullock labour may be deployed in preparatory tillage, repeated ploughing etc.

Other inputs

4.10.   We comment only very briefly here on inputs, apart from human and bullock labour, as they are not quantitatively very significant. Seeds, manures and fertilizers, irrigation and other charges, depreciation and interest charges are recorded among current (operational) inputs in the FMS. The seed rate per acre is influenced more by the method of sowing, climatic factors and level of irrigation than by the size of holdings as such. Manures and fertilizers constitute a small part of the expenditure. The amount of manure applied on smaller holdings is extremely small, as cattle dung, which is an important source of manure, is not available in adequate quantities and part of it is utilised as fuel. It was found during the years under study that chemical fertilizers were not much used and were used mostly on large holdings in the production of some selected crops; importantly, cash crops where irrigation is available (like American cotton in Punjab). No systematic relation between the expenditure on seeds, manures and fertilizers, and irrigation charges per acre, on the one hand, and size of holding, on the other, could be found.[3]

Machinery and implements

4.11.   The figures for value of implements and machinery, as well as those for 'fixed capital' (which includes residential housing, wells, farm buildings etc.) are very shaky. However, data are available in the FMS about distribution of agricultural implements by type and number. During the period under study no major changes were noticed by way of new implements. Implements are classified as 'traditional' and 'improved'.[4] It was found that in most regions there were not many users of improved implements, the performance varying greatly between regions in terms of value as well as type of implements. Table 4.II gives the value of implements on an average for each size class, per acre. In Punjab, improved implements were not un-known even on holdings of less than 5 acres, while in Madhya Pradesh they were found only on holdings above 10 acres. In U.P. and Bombay, although some of the improved implements (like the iron plough) were found on smaller holdings, the advantage (in terms of better implements and value of implements) definitely with the larger holdings. Due partly to indivisibilities of fixed capital assets, the *per acre* investment in implements and machinery shows an inverse trend with size of holding. This obviously cannot be interpreted as any relative advantage that the small cultivators enjoy.

3   The relation was positive for some years and negative for others and if statistically significant in one year was not so in another.

4   The 'traditional' implements consist of the iron plough, the hoe, the sickle, the harrow etc. while 'improved' implements include fodder cutters, carts with pneumatic tyres, iron crushers, furrow turning ploughs, Layalpur hoes, bar harrows, seed drills, chaff cutters, Persian wheels, etc.

Total value of inputs per acre

4.12. The FMS gives the total value of inputs per acre, defined as actual operational costs incurred together with the imputed costs for owned inputs (like family labour and imputed rent on owned land), according to size of holding. Although it covers all the material inputs entering production, the procedure of imputing costs at prevailing market rates to owned inputs is questionable. As we have pointed out in regard to labour input (see chapter 3), it is a dubious practice to treat the wage rate as an opportunity cost of family labour and thus implicitly assume that decisions concerning owned inputs are made on the basis of such a premise. We have given the figures for total costs per acre here only to note that, like bullock labour and investment inputs, total inputs *per acre* (of which these constitute a sizable part) show a systematic inverse relation with average size of holding.

4.13. To sum up, the variations in use of inputs over different holdings arise primarily from differences in the intensity of cultivation and cropping pattern. The characteristics of markets — more particularly, land, labour and output — and the resource position of cultivators, have an immediate influence on the intensity of cultivation and cropping pattern. To cite an example, we have already seen in Chapter 3 how the peculiarities of the labour market as well as the size of holding influence labour-use on different holdings. Our discussion of irrigation below (in Chapter 5) will further elucidate the point. Similarly we have tried to explain variations in bullock labour use, mainly in the light of the ownership distribution of bullocks and the cropping pattern. However, above all, shaping the characteristics of markets, the resource position of various groups of peasantry as well as the nature and the extent of their involvement in markets themselves, is the nexus of property relations. In our discussion of tenurial conditions we suggest provisional hypotheses on some aspects of property relations. The treatment is bound to be cursory given the nature of our information on these aspects.

5
Effects of irrigation

5.1.   Using the rather limited information available in the published FMS, we shall in this section develop a few ideas bearing on the effects of irrigation. The general level of irrigation in the regions under study is rather low, except in the case of Punjab and U.P., as is evident from Table 5.I. What is important furthermore, the quality and the nature of irrigation facilities show wide variations over regions depending upon the sources of irrigation. The major sources are canals (state and private), tanks, wells and tubewells. The relative efficiency of these varies remarkably; whereas tubewells and canal irrigation are relatively more dependable, tank and well irrigation is extremely sensitive to rainfall conditions, being essentially rainfed. Even within one type of irrigation there are wide differences in quality; wells can vary in depth, in construction — they can be lined with masonry or unlined. The efficiency of irrigation thus depends upon the quantum, regularity and controllability of water supply. The indicators used in the FMS, namely 'the percentage area irrigated of a holding' or 'the percentage number of holdings irrigated' in a region, cannot adequately reflect the nature or the extent of the facility.

Sources and level of irrigation

5.2.   In Table 5.I, we have noted the sources and level of irrigation in different regions. While state-built canals and private wells are the major sources of irrigation in all regions, there are very wide variations among them in the level of irrigation, partly because some are favoured with better rainfall conditions. Even so, given the uncertainty of rains, irrigation remains crucial in all regions. Punjab and U.P. are relatively better irrigated, the net area irrigated by all sources in Amritsar and Ferozepur in Punjab being 83 and 63 per cent of the net sown area respectively, compared with 62 and 57 per cent for Meerut and Muzaffarnagar in U.P. Irrigation in both these areas is supplied mainly by canals. In Madras State, Salem and Coimbatore had 15.2 and 22.9 per cent of net sown area irrigated, the predominant source of supply being wells. Bombay fared worse with only 7.5 per cent of the net sown area irrigated in Ahmednagar and 3.6 per cent in Nasik, again dependent mainly upon wells[1], while West Bengal had only around 6 per cent in one district and 45 per

1 An interesting observation emerging from the village statistics relating to Bombay is that usually the number of wells is higher in villages where the canal system is provided by the state. The reason could be partly technical; with water storage systems in the vicinity, wells work more efficiently. It could be partly due to the relative prosperity of the region in the hinterland of the canal system. It would be interesting to investigate the question whether government investment stimulates private investment or whether government investment

Table 5.I   *Sources and level of irrigation*

State/district	Sources (per cent of area irrigated):					Irrigated area to net sown area
	Wells	Tanks	Canals (state)	Canals (private)	Misc.	
	%	%	%	%	%	%
West Bengal						
Hooghly	–	51.93	33.95	–	14.12	45.46
24 Paraganas	3.94	93.24	2.82	–	–	5.97
U.P.						
Meerut	44.9	0.1	54.5	0.1	0.4	61.50
Muzaffarnagar	29.7	0.1	69.7	0.2	0.3	56.31
Bombay						
Ahmednagar	58.0	7.0	38.8	0.2	3.0	8.9
Nasik	59.0	2.0	36.4	0.6	2.0	5.7
Madras						
Salem	56.61	27.61	9.08	0.9	6.60	15.0
Coimbatore	72.30	6.20	18.40	–	3.15	25.3
Punjab						
Amritsar	37.0	N.A.	63.0	–	–	86.0
Ferozepur	11.0	N.A.	82.0	–	7.0	65.0
M.P.	negligible					

cent in another, of the net sown area irrigated, dependent mainly upon wells. At the extreme was Madhya Pradesh with virtually no irrigation, crop production being almost entirely rain dependent.

Intersize differences in irrigation

5.3.   A hypothesis to which we referred, in the context of the higher per acre value productivity on smaller holdings (see Chapter 2), maintains that the smaller farms generally have a higher percentage of their area irrigated as compared with the larger. Relating percentage area irrigated to the average size of holding we found that in Madras, the Hooghy district of West Bengal, Bombay and U.P. there was a statistically significant inverse relation (see Appendix G). In the cases of 24 Paraganas of West Bengal and Punjab (except for Amritsar in 1955–56) the relation was inverse but statistically not significant. In Madhya Pradesh there was very little irrigation in the two districts. A word of caution needs to be put in here about interpreting the average statistics. In the Madras Report (where, in addition to the information concerning percentage of area irrigated on an average in the size group, we also obtain information about the number of irrigated holdings in the group) we find that the percentage of holdings irrigated increases with the size group of holding, so that there

1(continued)
   usually favours regions which have economically better off cultivators. An attempt along
   these lines has been made by S.K. Rao (1972). For a detailed historical account of the
   construction of canal systems and their effects on well irrigation, see Elizabeth Whitcombe
   (1971).

41

is a larger proportion of unirrigated holdings in the smaller size groups,[2] while the percentage of area irrigated on an average is higher in these groups.

5.4. The question arises why there are greater irrigational facilities available on smaller holdings. Two not necessarily independent hypotheses may be advanced: firstly, that better irrigated regions end up with a smaller average size of holding, and secondly, that the smaller operators create and maintain irrigational facilities on their farms. To take up the first, better irrigated regions may be subject to a higher degree of fragmentation and subdivision of farms due to the population pressure that generally exists in such regions. Also the feasibility of a smaller economically viable unit, when irrigated, may stimulate this process. For example, the Report on Bombay (1954–57, p.6) observes that a close association existed between the average size of holding and the irrigational facility in villages, the better irrigated villages generally having a predominance of smaller size holdings and hence a lower average size. The population factor however may not be as forceful an explanation when we are comparing, cross-sectionally, holdings in the same village, and the other argument may hold, namely, that the economic viability of a smaller unit of cultivation when irrigated may lead to subdivision of an irrigated farm. Another factor also may operate when irrigated land is being leased out by a big landlord. The landlord may prefer parcelling out the irrigated land among very small tenants for two reasons: while his bargaining position remains strong *vis-à-vis* the petty tenant, the latter may also have to resort to very intensive cultivation in order to eke a subsistence out of the small plot leased to him. Thus the landlord may find it possible to maximize his returns (as a share of the total *gross* output on his entire land) if he leases out the land in smaller plots. This hypothesis cannot be tested here but is suggested as being a likely situation.

5.5. These, however, are explanations on the basis of historically available irrigation facilities. As both construction and maintenance of irrigation require labour, it may be argued that the smaller operators are in a favourable position to deploy their relatively larger family labour for such activities. They may do so particularly because they are hard-pressed to achieve the maximum output from the land. Relating the percentage area irrigated to earners per acre, we find (see Appendix G) that there is indeed a significant positive association between the two. This result,

2   The figures are as follows:

Table 5.II   *Percentage holdings and area irrigated Madras (1956–1957)*

Size group (acres)	Holdings irrigated Actual (no)	Percent	Area irrigated Actual (acre)	Percent
0–2.5	22	61.1	22.38	40.1
2.5–5.0	38	69.1	73.46	36.3
5.0–7.5	36	83.7	95.28	36.7
7.5–10.0	18	90.0	63.33	36.3
10.0–15.0	19	82.6	63.98	12.6
15–20	10	90.9	24.15	12.6
20–25	6	100.0	21.00	16.6
25 & above	5	100.0	3.44	7.0

however, has to be cautiously interpreted and should not necessarily be attributed a causal significance. We have seen in Chapter 3 that the number of earners per acre is inversely related to the size of holding and so is the percentage area irrigated. This may explain the positive association between the proportion of area irrigated and earners per acre observed here. More direct information is needed to test whether the availability of family labour in fact acts as a stimulus to the creation of irrigational facilities.

Effects of irrigation

5.6. Irrigation can raise the productivity of land in three ways: by making possible multiple cropping, by increasing the yield per unit cost and by making possible the production of more lucrative crops. Irrigation not being as widespread and effective in all regions, the relation between the intensity of cultivation and the percentage area irrigated turns out to be statistically not very significant (see Appendix G). As pointed out in the Madras Report,[3] irrigation, while making possible the production of lucrative crops, may yet not be adequate for multiple cropping. It would appear therefore that given the present level and quality of irrigation it makes its major contribution through increasing the yield per acre and allowing the production of more lucrative crops.

5.7. Reports on Punjab provide some information concerning holdings classified as irrigated and unirrigated. From Table 5.IIIA relating to Punjab, we notice a sub-stantially higher use of inputs (human and bullock labour as well as total inputs) per acre on irrigated as compared with unirrigated holdings. Human labour per acre almost doubles and so does the total cost of inputs (owned and imputed). Output per acre also shows a remarkable rise. Defining ΔO as the difference between yields per acre on irrigated and unirrigated holdings and ΔC as the difference in the total cost of inputs per acre within the same size group, we computed the 'incremental' output-input ratio for each size group, i.e. $\Delta O/\Delta C$ (see Table 5.IIIA). This increases systematically with the average size of holding suggesting that the 'relative gain' (as measured by $\Delta O/\Delta C$) through irrigation is higher on larger holdings.[4] Comparing the ratio of bullock labour with human labour by size of holding, it is seen that the ratio is higher on irrigated holdings (as compared with unirrigated ones) in all size groups suggesting a relatively greater use on these.

5.8. With regard to Madras and Bombay we have some information about holdings aggregated according to 'levels of irrigation' (see Table 5.IIIB). Both regions are mostly dependent upon wells and the efficiency of irrigation is rather low. The average size of holding is generally smaller at higher levels of irrigation. With respect to Bombay we notice that costs per acre, in cash as well as total (i.e. paid out *and* imputed), increase steeply with the rising level of irrigation. So also does the output

---

3 Madras Report (1956–57); p. 38.

4 This comparison has the limitation that we are not observing the difference made by irrigation to a previously unirrigated holding, but comparing two independent sets of holdings within the same size-groups.

Table 5.IIIA *Comparison of irrigated and unirrigated holdings: Punjab*

Size of holdings (acres)	Total input per acre (Rs)		Output per acre (Rs)		Bullock labour days per acre (days)		Human labour days per acre (days)		Bullock labour days / Human labour days		$\dfrac{\Delta O}{\Delta C}$
	Irrigated holdings	Unirrigated holdings	Irrigated holdings	Unirrigated holdings	Irrigated holdings	Unirrigated holdings	Irrigated holdings	Unirrigated holdings	Irrigated holdings	Unirrigated holdings	
0–5	247	142	207	150	19	14	24	12	0.77	1.14	0.54
5–10	216	112	197	109	19	15	24	13	0.78	1.09	0.84
10–20	205	99	201	79	18	13	24	13	0.76	0.97	1.14
20–50	188	85	194	74	16	10	23	11	0.79	0.96	1.16
50 and above	140	61	161	43	13	10	18	8	0.69	1.20	1.49

Table 5.IIIB Inputs and output per acre on holdings classified by level of irrigation

State/district level of irrigation	Paid out costs (Rs)		Total cost (cash and imputed) (Rs)		Output (Rs)		Farm business income (Rs)		Profit or loss (Rs)		Average size of holding (acres)	
	Ahmed-nagar	Nasik	Ahmed-nagar	Nasik	Ahmed-nagar	Nasik	Ahmed-nagar	Nasik	Ahmed-nagar	Nasik	Ahmed-nagar	Nasik
Bombay												
Completely unirrigated	18.8	22.9	34.5	43.5	37.0	39.0	18.2	16.1	2.5	−4.5	18.2	17.3
0–25%	23.8	41.6	44.3	72.6	46.2	73.9	22.4	32.3	1.9	1.3	27.6	21.6
25–50%	41.9	92.7	76.9	146.3	89.2	152.0	47.3	59.3	12.3	5.7	22.6	11.8
50–75%	88.1	251.7	140.9	344.1	129.3	242.8	41.2	8.9	−11.6	−101.3	14.8	6.3
75–100%	158.4	—	213.0	—	251.2	—	92.8	—	38.2	—	14.0	—
Completely irrigated	182.1	—	279.1	—	250.9	—	68.7	—	−28.3	—	4.7	—
Madras												
Fully unirrigated	64.9		92.3		91.0		31.0		3.6		4.6	
20–30%	2.3		152.3		149.7		68.1		7.9		6.0	
45–55%	145.2		259.7		350.0		209.9		95.4		7.5	
70–80%	245.9		392.9		405.0		172.5		25.5		3.9	
Fully irrigated	241.4		433.9		609.5		399.3		206.8		9.2	

per acre. *Farm business income* (defined as gross output minus paid out costs) *per acre* rises with higher levels of irrigation, but not consistently, being much less on the completely irrigated holdings than on the preceding group with 75 to 100 per cent area irrigated. It may be noted that the former group has a much smaller average size of holding as compared with the latter and this may constitute a relative disadvantage when levels of irrigation are not too far apart. In Madras, too, the inputs per acre and output per acre increased systematically with the level of irrigation. Again, profits per acre in the category of holdings having 70–80 per cent area irrigated were seen to be lower than on those with 45–55 per cent irrigated. In this case, too, the average size of holding for the former category was much lower (3.0 acres) compared with that for the latter (7.5 acres).

5.9.   Thus it appears that irrigation, while increasing productivity per acre, does so by making feasible intensive application of other inputs, the latter quite often increasing more than proportionately with the increase in output (i.e. $\Delta O/\Delta C < 1$). This may be partly due to the low quality of irrigation itself. Punjab, which has a better system of irrigation, shows more than proportionate returns on larger holdings. This suggests that the larger holdings when comparably irrigated may have an advantage in terms of per acre productivity or at least do not suffer from a disadvantage compared with the smaller. With the very aggregative information available here, it is not possible to substantiate this hypothesis rigorously.[5]

5.10.   One way to assess the influence irrigation may have on the relations between per acre input use (also input productivity) and the size of holding is to work out the relations separately for irrigated and unirrigated holdings and compare the results. Using the data for Punjab we find (see Appendix G) that the yield per acre continues to be inversely related to the average size of holding in both categories — but while the relation is statistically significant for *unirrigated* holdings, it is not so for the *irrigated* ones, except in 1956–57 when we still find the inverse relation weaker for the irrigated holdings. There appears to be no significant difference between the two categories of holdings when total inputs per acre are related to the size of holding. On the other hand, we note that the inverse relation between bullock labour days per acre and the size of holding appears to be stronger on *irrigated* holdings suggesting that the use of bullock labour is relatively more accentuated on smaller holdings when they are irrigated. A similar exercise with respect to Ahmednagar and Nasik in Bombay did not give consistent results for the two districts (see Appendix G). Both the extent and quality of irrigation in the two districts are rather poor and hence no conclusive observations can be made.

5.11.   We may roughly infer from the above that if irrigation is evenly spread over the different size-classes of holdings the 'inverse' tendency noticed in the relation

5   For Bombay and Punjab it was also possible to compare input utilisation and yield per acre between a crop when irrigated and when not. It can be seen (see Table 5.IV) that while yield per acre was higher when the crop was irrigated, inputs were even higher, so that the ratio of 'incremental output' to 'incremental input' (i.e. difference in yield per acre divided by differences in total inputs per acre) was less than one on all size-groups of holdings. We did not find that the size of holding had any relation to the additional yield per acre obtained by irrigating a crop.

Table 5.IV Comparison of irrigated and unirrigated crop: inputs and output per acre

State/size (acres) Bombay	Jowar: Ahmednagar				Wheat: Ahmednagar				Wheat: Nasik			
	ΔH (days)	ΔB (days)	ΔC (Rs)	$\frac{\Delta O}{\Delta C}$	ΔH (days)	ΔB (days)	ΔC (Rs)	$\frac{\Delta O}{\Delta C}$	ΔH (days)	ΔB (days)	ΔC (Rs)	$\frac{\Delta O}{\Delta C}$
Below 5	36.3	12.8	68.2	6.4	28.1	32.6	55.8	0.57	24.8	22.5	44.6	0.04
5–10	27.1	31.2	49.7	10.5	40.6	53.4	82.9	0.06	36.4	54.6	106.7	0.03
10–15	22.9	24.3	68.2	5.4	27.6	31.1	88.2	0.03	53.2	56.5	118.1	0.04
15–20	22.3	33.2	45.8	6.0	31.8	42.2	34.5	0.07	52.3	53.7	146.7	0.02
20–25	31.5	30.0	71.3	7.9	32.0	33.8	39.7	0.05	55.6	63.3	146.2	0.05
25–30	29.9	31.7	39.4	5.6	32.2	58.7	76.2	0.01	42.1	52.2	114.8	0.05
30–50	20.0	27.2	43.5	8.0	7.5	17.7	37.2	0.03	34.9	48.3	84.3	0.01
50 & above	23.8	11.6	38.2	6.7	14.2	32.8	81.8	0.10	29.1	26.4	71.2	−0.01
Punjab	Wheat – gram											
0–5	4.5	3.7	27.4	0.08								
5–10	6.1	3.2	25.5	0.07								
10–20	4.0	4.2	30.1	0.07								
20–50	5.8	5.6	38.5	0.06								
50 & above	2.7	−0.8	26.8	0.11								

Note: ΔH = Difference between human labour days per acre spent on the crop when irrigated and when not

ΔB = Difference between bullock labour days per acre spent on the crop when irrigated and when not

ΔC = Difference between total costs per acre spent on the crop when irrigated and when not

ΔO = Difference between output per acre when the crop is irrigated and when not

between productivity of land and farm size may tend to be weakened. It is likely, furthermore, that a well-irrigated large holding with its relative superiority in terms of financial power to provide complementary assets and inputs may even obtain a differential advantage. The hypothesis calls for holding-wise data covering an adequately large sample of holdings with comparable levels of irrigation but differing in size. In the Report on Bombay (1955–56) holding-wise data are available according to the 'level of tenancy' (defined in terms of percentage of total area leased in) and 'the level of irrigation' (defined in terms of percentage of net sown area irrigated).[6] Information on yield per acre, returns on farming and costs per acre is available for each holding. Classifying the holdings according to each combination of a particular level of tenancy and of irrigation (e.g. wholly owned and wholly irrigated denoted by [A, O] and likewise [B, O] and so on) we studied the relation between yield per acre and the size of holding.[7] Except for the class of unirrigated and purely owned holdings in Ahmednagar and for the class of those irrigated up to 25 per cent of area and wholly owned in Nasik, we found no systematic inverse relation between yield per acre and the size of holding. (See Appendix G.) It would thus appear that the inverse relation cannot be generalised without reservations for holdings with comparable levels of irrigation and tenancy.

Irrigation and cropping pattern

5.12.   Irrigation also contributes to raising the productivity of land by making possible production of lucrative crops. For example, on irrigated holdings in Punjab only 50 per cent of the cropped area was devoted to food crops with 25 per cent under fodder and 20 per cent under cotton (American and *Desi*). On unirrigated holdings, on the other hand, wheat gram was the main crop with 73–94 per cent of cropped area going to food crops. In Madras where the quality of irrigation is poor, multiple cropping is not widely prevalent and food crops predominate on all holdings. But the irrigated holdings concentrate on paddy, a relatively more valuable crop, while the unirrigated holdings mainly produce dry grains like *Cumbu* and *Cholam*.

5.13.   Incidentally, it may be noted here that the relation between changes in relative prices of outputs and the cropping pattern appears to be somewhat different in the predominantly dry areas from that in better irrigated areas. The data we have are not only too aggregative in terms of size-classes but also cover only three years so that this hypothesis can only be suggested here as a tentative one. It would appear that in predominantly dry areas shifts in cropping patterns take place mainly in response to climatic conditions and that these shifts, via availability of output, influence relative prices. In Ahmednagar–Nasik region, for example, variations between

6   There are five levels of tenancy: (A) purely owned holdings (B) holdings with up to 25 per cent area leased-in (C) those with 25 to 50 per cent area leased-in (D) those with 50–75 per cent area leased-in (E) those with above 70 per cent area leased-in. The levels of irrigation are also stratified in five groups: (0) wholly unirrigated holdings (1) holdings with up to 25 per cent area irrigated (2) those with 25–50 per cent area irrigated (3) those with 50–75 per cent area irrigated and (4) those with above 75 per cent area irrigated.

7   In some classes, e.g. (D, 0) or (E, 0), there were too few observations to carry out such an exercise. See Appendix G.

Jowar and *Bajri* depend upon the expected rainfall conditions at the time of sowing. If the rains are expected to be poor – or do not arrive in time – the cultivators prefer to sow the hardier crop, *Jowar,* which requires much less watering. This allocation of·area is reflected in post-harvest relative prices. The previous year's prices did not seem to influence the allocation of area to crops. Wheat, which is grown on the irrigated tracts in the same region, is reported to have had very small variations in acreage. Of course, three years is too short a period to build up any lagged relation (as it ought to be) in order to study area-responses. The weak response of cropping pattern to prices in the case of an unirrigated area may perhaps be explained as follows. The yield of the crop depends on climatic conditions. The cropping pattern is decided in advance and costs incurred, the return to which depends ultimately upon the regularity of the seasonal cycles. Since prices depend primarily upon the state of the crop at the time of the harvest they are as uncertain as the climatic conditions themselves. Therefore, it is not so much the past year's relative prices as anticipations regarding the behaviour of the climatic factor at the time of sowing that influence the cropping pattern. Of course a persistent price trend in one. direction could have effects on the cropping pattern especially if the competing crops are not very different in their water requirement.

5.14.   The pattern in regions of assured irrigation could be different. So far as the dominant influence of the climatic factor is somewhat circumscribed and the risk of crop failure considerably reduced, it may be expected that farm operators will respond to changes in relative prices. Greater versatility in production is also possible so that cultivation can easily be shifted from one crop to another. Further, general economic conditions in such areas are bound to be better than in the unirrigated or low-irrigated regions, rendering profitable the production on a commercial scale of lucrative crops like superior grains, fruit, vegetables etc., adding to the range of possible crop-mixes. There is a growing literature on the question of area responses to changes in relative prices.[8] We have touched upon this issue in passing only to refer to a possible effect of irrigation.

5.15.   Thus we notice that, in general, the smaller holdings are relatively better irrigated. This may come about due to several factors: either because irrigated holdings get relatively more fragmented or are leased out in small plots to petty tenants by landowners who wish to maximize their return; or, because the smaller operators create and maintain irrigational facilities to cultivate their small holdings as intensively as possible. We further note that inputs per acre are considerably higher on the irrigated holdings (or irrigated crops) as compared with unirrigated holdings (or unirrigated crops) and often the difference in input cost per acre outweighs the value of the difference in output per acre, especially on very small holdings. This possibly occurs because the small operators are interested in securing as large a *gross* output per acre as possible rather than in maximizing *net* output per acre. Further, we find some ground to expect that the inverse relation between per acre productivity and size of holding may be somewhat weakened if irrigation

8   See, among others, Krishna R. (1963), Narain D. (1965), Krishna J. and Rao M.S. (1965).

is evenly spread out over all sizes of holdings. Irrigation influences cropping pattern, too, widening the range of production possibilities, particularly through making possible production of lucrative crops. The cropping patterns appear to be more responsive to price variations in irrigated areas than in the unirrigated areas.

6
Note on tenurial conditions

Types of tenancy

6.1.   Tenurial conditions in India vary markedly from region to region and within regions. The information recorded in the FMS is extremely scanty and is based on a quantitative index of the 'level of tenancy' as measured by the proportion of land leased-in to the size of holding and on broad categories of tenure. These notes are therefore necessarily incomplete and suggestive and do not come anywhere near to being a thorough enquiry.

6.2.   Holdings can be classified broadly as wholly owned, partially rented (i.e. when land is leased-in to supplement own holding) and fully rented holdings. Further, the terms on which land is leased-in can be broadly classified into three categories: fixed *kind* rent (i.e. a quantity of produce *in kind* is fixed as rent irrespective of the harvested output), fixed cash rent and share cropping. Under the last, a certain share of the harvested produce goes to the landlord. Within these broad categories there can be any number of variations in details; for example, the landlord providing or loaning a part of the inputs or the tenant supplying all the current inputs. The terms on which produce is shared between the landlord and the petty tenant can be quite onerous for the latter. Although there is a legislative upper limit to the share accruing to the landlord, the legal restrictions are rarely enforced. Furthermore, the tenancy rights continue to be quite insecure despite legislation. On the one hand, the tenants could be tenants-at-will who can be forced off the land by the landlord without compensation or notice. On the other hand, the tenant could be held virtually in bondage particularly if the landlord can also impose terms on the time and mode of repayment of debts. He can so choose the time for repayment or fix the prices of the crop when the repayment is in kind so that he can procure very high rates of usury. The landlord often extracts from the tenant free or underpaid labour services on his farm. Thus, as noted in 1.8 above, the markets (land, credit, labour and output) get closely interlocked. The petty tenant, given his inferior economic position in the rural nexus, finds his *feasible* choices in the other markets curtailed simultaneously when he is being exploited in the land-lease market. Neither the 'level of tenancy' nor the broad categories of legal forms of contracts capture the manner in which land, output, labour and credit markets become interlocked by the relative bargaining position of the various rural classes. Knowledge concerning these details is particularly relevant in view of the fact that land is leased-in not only by small cultivators but also by large owners. In fact ,

Table 6.I, which gives the data on the proportion of owned to total operated size of holding for Bombay and West Bengal, reveals no systematic relation with the size of holding and indicates that large holdings also lease-in a considerable proportion of their area.[1]

Table 6.I *Proportion of owned to total cultivated area*

State/size (acres)	%	%
Bombay	Ahmednagar	Nasik
Below 5	90	89
5−10	92	87
10−15	86	80
15−20	80	92
20−25	83	83
25−30	89	80
30−50	80	75
50 and above	75	80
West Bengal	Hooghly	24 Paraganas
0.01−1.25	85	67
1.26−2.50	78	75
2.50−3.75	62	70
3.75−5.00	60	75
5.00−7.50	67	76
7.50−10.00	62	90
10−15	86	76
Above 15	100	66

6.3   The tenurial systems as historically evolved in the various regions differ markedly. After tenancy reform bills were introduced in the sixties, concealed tenancy became widespread so that 'purely owned' or 'self cultivated' holdings appear to be the predominant recorded category everywhere. In Punjab, owner-cultivated land forms about 70 per cent of land operated, other types of tenancies being cash rent (about 11 per cent of land operated), kind rent (about 5 per cent) and share rent (about 1 per cent of land operated). In West Bengal, while fully owned farms account for 61 per cent of the total number of farms, nearly two fifths depend partly or wholly on leased-in land under share cropping. Under the latter system about half of the gross produce is the share of the land owner and the tenant has no rights on land. In Bombay, about 78 per cent of holdings are self-cultivated, the most prevalent system of tenant-cultivation being crop-sharing (about 14 per cent of holdings). The Bombay Report states that, although, by law the landlord cannot take more than one-fourth of the output in the case of irrigated and one-sixth in the case of dry crops, the commonly prevalent share is as high as fifty per cent of the crop. In the U.P. the predominant tenures as reported are *Bhumidari* (with 74 per cent area under it) and *Sirdari* (about 24 per cent of area). Under the latter, the cultivator has a transferable right on land and enjoys freedom from eviction, while *Bhumidari* ensures only occupancy right without

1   For a number of interesting hypotheses concerning the working of the lease markets see
    K.N. Raj (1970).

52

right of transfer and the *Bhumidar* is liable to ejection. The third type of tenant, *Assami*, is a non-occupancy tenant who can be thrown off the land on any number of legally defensible grounds. The U.P. Report states that after the abolition of Zamindari, and tenancy reforms, land rights have been transferred to tenants. However, as mentioned earlier, the legal position can be significantly at variance with actual conditions. In Madras the self-cultivated area formed about 80 per cent of the cultivated area, the area leased on cash rent about 12 per cent, that on kind rent about 2 per cent and that under crop-sharing about 5 per cent. In Madhya Pradesh the owner cultivated, cash rented and share rented lands formed 70, 16 and 14 per cent respectively of the total cultivated area.

Economic performance in relation to 'level' and types of tenancy

6.4.   The Punjab Report classifies holdings as 'owned', 'fixed or cash rented' lands and 'share rented or *Batai*'. The percentage area irrigated is found to be higher, on an average, on owned and cash rented holdings than on share-rented (see Table 6.II). The difference becomes more prominent on the larger holdings. If this observation has a more general validity (our information here is admittedly inadequate), two possible hypotheses, or a combination of them, can be suggested. The first is that those tenants who can secure land on the basis of a fixed rent system have a greater incentive to undertake the provision and maintenance of irrigational facilities. This, however, appears unlikely unless the lease is a secure long term one with the level of fixed rent remaining constant or changing predictably. If the tenant has a relatively weaker bargaining position or he is a tenant-at-will so that the landlord can deprive him of his tenurial rights, he will have very little incentive to undertake investment in irrigation or in other such durable assets which are not shiftable. The second explanation appears the more likely one: namely that, for the tenant, a fixed rent contract on already irrigated land may appear more attractive as he can then exploit the full economics of irrigation which requires an intensive application of his own inputs, particularly labour. It may ordinarily be expected that the landlord, in view of the possibilities of intensive cultivation, will prefer crop-sharing where he can secure a proportionate share of the potential gain. In fact, the landlord can adopt two alternative strategies; (a) he can lease the land on a crop-sharing basis, with the possible risk that the tenant, under crop sharing, may not be willing to apply as much labour and other inputs as he would under a fixed-rent contract, or (b) he may fix a rent under a fixed rent contract which is high enough to capitalise the higher land productivity; the fixity of rent may yet provide the incentive to the tenant to cultivate the land intensively and thereby make use of the irrigation potential as well as maintain the facilities. If the tenurial contract is not secure and long-term, the landlord can raise rents and capitalise the productivity gains for each new tenant or for the same tenant under the threat of ejection. This strategy will work even better if the landlord parcels out his land in such small units that the tenant has to cultivate the small piece of land intensively to raise enough crop to provide his subsistence after paying the landlord's share. We have seen in Chapter 5 that, particularly on small holdings, inputs are applied at a very high rate on an irrigated holding as compared to an unirrigated one in the same

Table 6.II   *Tenancy and land use: Punjab*

Types of tenancy Size of holdings (acres)	Self-cultivated and cash-rented	Share-rented
I. Percentage area irrigated	(%)	(%)
0–5	92	90
5–10	91	82
10–20	84	73
20–50	73	63
50 and above	94	74
II. Intensity of cropping		
0–5	164	150
5–10	159	136
10–20	140	128
20–50	124	123
50 and above	110	104
III. Cropping pattern (percentage area cultivated)		
Food crops	60	63
Oilseeds	3	2
Fibre crops	16	16
Fodder crops	21	18
Misc. crops	–	1

size-class although the increases in output are less than proportionate. The small tenants, driven by their need to extract subsistence, could be maximising the *gross* output from the land and, while the fixed rent is an incentive for them to apply inputs intensively, it may enable the landlord to capitalise these gains by fixing the level of the rent at a high enough rate. This is a hypothesis which needs to be tested on a more detailed informational basis than is available here. We do, however, have some evidence which is not in conflict with the hypothesis that tenants under fixed rent cultivate the land more intensively. Intensity of cropping is found to be system-atically higher for all size-groups in the 'owned and fixed rent' tenancy group as compared to the cash rent category. The higher proportion of irrigated area under the former may partly explain this. However, with the increasing average size of holding over the size-classes, while the differences in intensity of cultivation between the two tenurial systems narrow down, the differences in percentage area irrigated become more marked. Thus irrigation does not seem to be the only factor; the incentive to use land intensively appears to be greater on owner operated lands and on lands under fixed rent than under crop-sharing tenancy.

6.5.   In Chapter 5 we referred to the holding-wise information available in respect to Bombay for the year 1955–56 according to levels of irrigation and tenancy (see 5.10). Classifying the information in the form of two-way tables (see Tables 6.III, A-E) we tabulated the group averages for size of holding, total cost per acre, *farm business income*[2] per acre and output per acre for each combination of the 'level of tenancy' and 'level of irrigation'. We observe that for Ahmednagar, the total cost

---

2   *Farm business income* is defined as gross value of output minus paid-out costs.

per acre (average for the group) generally shows an increase with the level of irrigation for each 'level of tenancy'. While the differences in costs per acre among the various levels of tenancy are not so predominant at lower levels of irrigation (i.e. unirrigated and irrigated up to 25 per cent area), the costs differ substantially at higher levels of irrigation. This may perhaps be explained as follows: generally speaking, when an operator has to share part of the produce with the landlord or pay kind or cash rent, it is possible that there is less of an incentive to apply his own (labour and other material) inputs intensively compared to the situation of an owner-cultivator. However, at lower levels of irrigation, the differences in intensity may be less; first, because lack of, or an inadequate supply of, irrigation itself restricts the scope for such an intensive application of inputs; second, whether land is irrigated or not, the tenant-cultivator may have inevitably to work the land intensively enough to be able to provide for an adequate level of output (possibly a subsistence level) after paying off the landlord's share. With higher levels of irrigation, the opportunities for intensive application of inputs grow and the owner-cultivators (or predominantly owner-cultivators) may invest more in production. Output per acre shows a consistent trend for Ahmednagar; it increases with the level of irrigation for each level of tenancy and decreases with the level of tenancy for each level of irrigation. In the case of Nasik, the level of costs as well as output per acre show no such consistent of systematic tendencies. This may arise partly because of the very small number of observations in the Nasik sample (smaller than in the case of Ahmednagar) at higher levels of irrigation, there being no holdings having more than than 75 per cent irrigated (see Table 6.III-A). Also, whereas the average size within each combination of the level of irrigation and tenancy shows no large or systematic differences in Ahmednagar, with regard to Nasik we find marked variations in the average size of holding. In any case, these comments, based as they are on a very limited number of observations, are at best tentative and suggestive.

6.6.   The reports on Punjab indicate that the tenurial system may have some influence on cropping patterns; the share-rented lands have a higher percentage area under food and less under cash crops as compared with owner-cultivated and fixed-rented holdings. It is possible that a share-cropper is reluctant to venture into the more profitable but risky crops which, incidentally, also generally require a high level of inputs since he has to share the profits with the landlord. This will be specially so if he has no direct access to output markets but has to sell the produce to intermediaries, to the moneylender or to the landlord himself, so that profitability is greatly reduced. The tenant would rather produce more food crops, requiring less inputs per acre but protecting his subsistence, than produce a cash crop which has to be disposed of in a market where his bargaining position is weak. It is also possible that, since cash crops require considerable amounts of inputs per acre (labour and other material inputs) and these inputs, especially labour, may have to be supplied by the tenant for reasons discussed above, the landlord may prefer to lease the land out on a fixed rent basis with a stipulation that rent be paid in kind in terms of the cash crop. All these are suggested as working hypotheses which need to be investigated. We need to know the full details of the tenurial contracts which vary widely not only from region to region but from holding to holding. These variations are bound to be significant and our observations with respect to Punjab

Table 6.III Ahmednagar and Nasik:

A. Distribution of holdings (no.)

Ahmednagar

Level of irrigation \ Level of tenancy	A	B	C	D	E
0	12	2	5	1	1
1	20	2	4	1	1
2	9	1	3	1	0
3	2	0	2	1	0
4	9	0	0	1	0

Nasik

Level of irrigation \ Level of tenancy	A	B	C	D	E
0	12	4	6	2	0
1	22	11	6	4	1
2	5	5	0	0	1
3	1	0	1	0	0
4	0	0	0	0	0

B. Average size of holding (acres)

Ahmednagar

Level of irrigation \ Level of tenancy	A	B	C	D	E
0	12.5	18.4	17.2	4.2	13.8
1	26.0	69.2	28.5	34.7	35.0
2	18.3	17.7	27.7	23.8	–
3	19.8	–	14.0	14.7	–
4	6.3	–	–	16.3	–

Nasik

Level of irrigation \ Level of tenancy	A	B	C	D	E
0	14.5	23.8	14.2	20.5	–
1	17.5	29.9	24.2	21.3	22.4
2	7.6	5.1	–	–	6.3
3	8.2	–	5.9	–	–
4	–	–	–	–	–

Table 6.III (continued)

C. Output per acre (Rs)

Ahmednagar

Level of irrigation \ Level of tenancy	A	B	C	D	E
0	38.6	37.3	34.7	16.5	24.1
1	37.8	46.7	36.7	33.2	22.7
2	86.8	87.4	71.9	29.4	–
3	132.2	–	65.1	49.4	–
4	189.3	–	–	115.9	–

Nasik

Level of irrigation \ Level of tenancy	A	B	C	D	E
0	42.8	34.2	38.5	44.3	–
1	72.0	78.3	53.4	64.5	97.5
2	184.6	195.7	–	–	76.3
3	149.2	–	249.9	–	–
4	–	–	–	–	–

D. Total costs per acre (Rs)

Ahmednagar

Level of irrigation \ Level of tenancy	A	B	C	D	E
0	39.7	42.7	39.6	50.4	17.7
1	41.7	39.8	41.9	36.1	24.6
2	90.6	67.1	70.9	45.5	–
3	167.6	–	95.3	87.1	–
4	222.9	–	–	145.4	–

Nasik

Level of irrigation \ Level of tenancy	A	B	C	D	E
0	44.4	35.2	45.8	28.3	–
1	76.5	66.2	51.4	64.5	78.6
2	139.3	215.2	–	–	104.6
3	170.0	–	275.8	–	–
4	–	–	–	–	–

Table 6.III (continued)

E. Farm business income per acre (Rs)

Ahmednagar

Level of irrigation \ Level of tenancy	A	B	C	D	E
0	17.3	14.6	9.4	−10.9	18.2
1	18.0	16.9	13.8	9.8	5.0
2	42.6	57.6	27.2	−8.1	−
3	10.2	−	8.0	−0.2	−
4	40.5	−	−	40.8	−

Nasik

Level of irrigation \ Level of tenancy	A	B	C	D	E
0	20.4	16.2	10.9	29.0	−
1	30.5	37.4	23.7	23.0	64.9
2	90.6	82.3	−	−	16.4
3	26.9	−	103.0	−	−
4	−	−	−	−	−

Table 6.IV   *Tenancy and cropping pattern: Madras (1956-57)*

Type of tenancy	Intensity of cropping	Proportion of area under: (per cent)						
		Paddy	Cholam	Ragi	Cumbu	Other crops	Cotton	Groundnut
Fully rented-in	0.71	8.5	7.9	7.5	39.1	29.5	11.2	1.3
Partially rented-in	1.13	9.2	21.3	21.3	11.7	31.1	6.5	8.7
Owner-cultivated	1.18	13.6	13.3	13.3	9.8	22.1	13.0	11.3

may not be generalisable. For example, in the jute belt of West Bengal it is customary for credit to be extended to share-cropping tenants for jute cultivation on terms stipulating repayment in kind. Share-cropping is a pervasive system in this area and most tenants producing jute are under the share-cropping system.

6.7.   For Madras we have information about cropping patterns on 'owner-cultivated' and 'tenant cultivated' holdings, the latter subdivided into 'partially' and 'fully' rented holdings, (see Table 6.IV). The fully rented holdings have a much lower intensity of cultivation as compared with the owner-cultivated and they appear to specialise rather heavily (devoting about 80 per cent of area) in food crops. Even among the food crops they concentrate on *cumbu*, a subsistence crop which is grown mostly for home consumption. The owner-cultivated and partially rented holdings, while also predominantly food-producing, show a greater diversification of production even among food crops. These are cursory observations. Detailed investigations into tenurial systems of individual regions, diverse as they are, are required before any generalisations can be attempted.

6.8.   Here, given the rather inadequate and partial information on tenancy, we have attempted to develop a few suggested hypotheses. There are very wide inter-regional variations in systems of tenancy so that our observations regarding any particular region may not be generalisable. Considering Punjab, we have attempted to explain why the holdings which are either owned or leased out on a fixed rent basis have a higher level of irrigation. This we have done mainly in terms of the landlord's expectation that the tenant will cultivate land more intensively, applying his own inputs, if he (the tenant) is to pay a fixed rent rather than a share of the crop. The landlord may be able to capitalise the productivity increases by fixing a high enough rent, raising it under the threat of eviction or bringing in a new tenant on a higher rent contract. We noted the rather different situation in West Bengal where the system of share-cropping was pervasive and bound closely with the credit system, the landlord also functioning as a money lender to the tenant. In the case of Bombay, we have two-way information about holdings classified according to levels of tenancy and levels of irrigation. We compared costs and returns between different levels of tenancy for comparable levels of irrigation and noted that with increasing levels of tenancy output per acre showed a tendency to decline. Also, at lower levels of tenancy, inputs were applied relatively more intensively.

We noted a few observations concerning the cropping patterns on different types of tenancy holdings. In Punjab, the share-rented holding devoted a larger percentage area to food-crops than the fixed-rented or ownership holdings. In West Bengal, however, share-cropping is pervasive and most tenants producing jute are also share-croppers. In Madras, while food production appears to be predominant on all types of holding, the owner-cultivated holding had a more diversified pattern within food crops and produced also a better variety of grains.

7
Cropping pattern and the size of holding

7.1.   We have indicated at several places in the preceding discussion that the cropping pattern, along with intensity of cropping, may explain a number of relations observed between input uses (and productivity) and the average size of holding which appear to hold for total crop production but fail to do so at the level of individual crops. We have also referred to the various resource constraints (or specific resource availabilities) which operate on different size-classes of holdings. There is a two-way relation between resources at the disposal of, or accessible to, a cultivator and his position in the factor and output markets of the rural economy: his initial resource constraints determine for him his bargaining position in the land and credit market (e.g. the terms on which he can lease in or lease out land and secure credit or loan out funds); they also determine his dependence on hiring in or out of labour or on purchase of other inputs. On the other hand his past and current involvements in market operations influence his production decisions and, through these, his future resource availabilities. For example, a heavily indebted sharecropper more or less loses the freedom to decide when, to whom and on what terms to dispose of his output; if, in addition, his tenancy is insecure, he can hardly improve his resource position by asset creation or through better productive performance. Thus, his bargaining strength in various markets affects the quanta of resources available to him and hence his production decisions as to how much land to lease out or lease in and on what terms, how much to invest in land, how intensively to cultivate it and what crops to grow, etc. Furthermore, the economic status of the cultivator and his position in the nexus of relations also define for him the objectives he sets himself to achieve. There are no motivational forces which are definable *a priori* for any operator independently of the entire gamut of production and market relations in which he is involved. Thus it is futile to reduce all operators to profit maximizers, drawing upon the analogy of capitalist producers in a competitive market economy. The FMS gives profits (losses) *per acre* in different size groups of holdings, calculated by netting the gross output for all costs – those actually incurred as well as costs imputed to owned inputs at market rates. These not only vary haphazardly from holding to holding but, what is more important, the majority of holdings come out with losses. The profit maximization hypothesis can be saved only by conceding that most farms are in a state of nonviability (the 'maximum' profits being negative) or that expectations of positive profits are in fact not fulfilled in the majority of cases. What is more plausible however is that, for a large number of cultivators, profit in this sense is not the relevant category at all. Total returns (including wages for family labour, rents on owned land), i.e. gross output netted for paid out costs, may be more

61

relevant. When the cultivator cannot even make both ends meet, it may not be the net returns but the gross yield which he seeks to maximize with the burden of debt allowed to accumulate. The 'motivational' forces at play are extremely complex and not enough research has yet gone into unravelling them.

Categories of cultivators

7.2.   Relying on the limited information here available, we present a rather over-simplified categorisation of cultivators into 'very small', 'small', 'middle' and 'large' which may be useful to focus on the conditions of production that are particular to these different groups. (The landless are not included here as the FMS covers farm operators). The very small farmers are, in their economic status, not far removed from the landless labourers as they too are dependent upon hiring out labour. Our discussion below of cropping patterns in relation to individual regions will broadly identify these groups for the region concerned. They cannot be identified precisely given the nature of the information we have and will vary in terms of the size range of holding from region to region, so that our general discussion does not specify the size range for each group.

7.3.   The 'very small' cultivators possess very little land relative to the available family labour and depend upon hiring out labour to supplement their income from land. The landless who lease-in a tiny piece of land in search of some secure income (see 3.6) fall into this category as well. Very often they possess no bullocks and have to hire their services for payment or in exchange for labour. They have quite often to purchase seeds; the gross output of the previous harvest may only just cover or even fall short of family consumption. Also, if they have debt liabilities, the output or a part of it may have to be disposed of soon after harvest for debt repayments. Quite often, they are compelled to raise consumption loans or even loans to provide circulating capital on onerous terms of repayment — the own rate of interest on such loans turns out to be very high. The rates of hire, whether of bullock labour or equipment, work out, on an average, higher for the very small farmers. We calculated the per hired day rate for bullock labour by the number of bullock days and found it to be higher on the very small holdings. This was the case with human labour too. As was observed earlier (see 3.13), even small holdings hire in casual labour for specific operations or in peak seasons. The explanation for the higher rate for both could be that during peak seasons when the very small farmers hire in these services, the rates are higher than at other times. With regard to labour, another reason could be the somewhat specialised nature of the operations for which labour may have to be hired. Furthermore, there could be diseconomies of buying inputs in smaller quantities. The dependence of this class on the market for providing circulating capital is reflected in the index of monetisation of inputs (proportion of inputs purchased) given in Table 7.I. We note that the dependence on cash expenditure is very high in their case. It declines for the holdings in the next highest size classes and picks up again on the large holdings. The higher index of monetisation of the large holdings is qualitatively a different phenomenon from that on the very small ones. While in the former case it reflects a higher degree of commercialisation of production, in the latter it is more a reflection of the distress conditions under which production is carried out and market involvement assumes a compulsive character.

Table 7.I   A. Extent of monetisation of inputs: West Bengal (1954–57)

Size of farms (acres)	Percentage of cash expenditure to total input		
	Hooghly	24 Paraganas	Districts combined
0.01–1.25	27.5	24.8	26.7
1.26–2.50	34.8	16.3	26.8
2.51–3.75	31.7	12.0	22.9
3.76–5.00	19.9	21.6	20.6
5.01–7.50	23.0	16.5	21.6
7.51–10.00	13.2	13.3	13.2
10.01–15.00	26.5	31.6	29.0
Above 15.00	47.9	8.4	33.9

B. Percentage of cash expenditure to total expenditure on various inputs: Madhya Pradesh

Size of holdings (acres)	Seed		Human labour		Bullock labour		Overall	
	1955–56	1956–57	1955–56	1956–57	1955–56	1956–57	1955–56	1956–57
0–5	81.9	86.7	93.3	80.0	60.4	66.9	77.1	71.1
5–10	81.9	72.7	85.4	70.8	52.3	53.5	67.5	64.0
10–15	62.8	87.8	87.4	70.2	44.4	41.2	65.4	60.8
15–20	75.5	63.1	95.7	76.8	35.6	37.5	63.1	55.6
20–30	63.4	66.2	90.4	77.2	24.0	35.7	54.3	51.5
30–40	50.1	50.8	83.9	73.7	24.1	36.1	52.1	51.4
40–50	55.0	61.6	83.7	74.3	44.4	36.9	68.8	57.5
50 and above	51.4	68.3	74.8	72.8	21.6	32.0	51.3	58.6

7.4.   Given their higher availability of family labour relative to land, it may be expected that these small farms will concentrate on the relatively more labour-absorbing crops. The intensity of cultivation is higher on these holdings which, as we saw in Chapter 4, means that their bullock use *per acre* is not lower as compared with others, and that they have to hire in a substantial part of it, if not the entire amount. Given their resource base, they are severely constrained by the need to raise cash resources even in order to keep the cycle of production going. This may explain why farmers in this group are seen to allocate a higher proportion of their area to more lucrative (i.e. yielding higher gross revenue per acre) although risky, cash crops, especially if the crops (like jute, groundnuts) require a high labour input per acre and do not require any specific investments in equipment etc. Also it is quite often possible to get credit more easily for cash crop production on the condition of re-payment in kind. Land can be more easily leased-in and circulating capital or a part of it borrowed from the landlord on a contract to raise a cash crop on the farm. For example, in West Bengal, the FMS reports that the holdings which produced cash crops *only* (constituting only one per cent of the total number of holdings) were concentrated in the very small size-groups. Our notes below on cropping pattern, separately for individual regions, bring out a similar feature of the cropping pattern in other regions as well. Part of the food requirements of the family may be earned as wage income since labour is hired out and wages are quite often paid in kind, and in any case, food crops may not yield the high rate of gross revenue per acre that cash crops do. Of course there is a greater risk attached to lack of self-sufficiency in food. But given the tiny size of the holding and given that even to raise the food crop he has to finance circulating capital through loans which he has to repay immediately after the harvest so that he may not be able to provide for consumption in the following periods, the operator has to depend on market purchases or on consumption commodity loans to feed the family through the year.

7.5.   The next group of 'small farmers' (with somewhat larger holdings) is also characterised by relatively higher availability of family labour. They are less dependent upon the purchase of operational inputs (as reflected in the lower extent of monetization of inputs; see Table 7.I) than the very small farmers and hence are under somewhat less pressure to raise cash resources. Employment outside the farm is much lower in their case (see Table 3.I) and they raise more of the subsistence food crops on the farm using family labour to cultivate the land.

7.6.   The next group of bigger holdings which may be called 'middle', are somewhat more self-sufficient in terms of bullock labour, seed requirements, equipment etc.; they have a higher level of irrigation than the 'large' holdings and generally produce a surplus over subsistence. In a note below (see Appendix H) we have attempted to measure the 'technical efficiency' of different size-classes of holdings in terms of an index based on multiple inputs. We find that the 'middle' group of holdings are 'technically' more efficient in the sense defined there; namely, under certain assumptions, they can be seen to be employing input combinations closer to the 'technically minimum combinations' for given output levels. They produce a crop-mix which covers a larger variety of crops; these are mainly food crops, but the more lucrative ones. These crops, like vegetables, require considerable care in weeding, sowing, transplanting etc. Unlike the first two groups of holdings — 'very small' and 'small' — where dependence on the market appears to be primarily a by-product of providing consumption requirements for the family (thus one could roughly characterise it as 'production for consumption' as distinguished from 'production for the market'), the middle farmers are producing, at least in part, for the market. Not all of the disposal of their output occurs under conditions of distress, at least during periods of normal climatic conditions.

7.7.   The 'large' holdings produce for the market, i.e. to raise a surplus. In poorly irrigated regions the 'large' holdings have, on an average, a lower level of irrigation than the smaller groups. Intensity of cultivation is much lower (see Chapter 5). They do not depend totally upon hired labour — family labour continuing to play an important role — although the proportion of hired to family labour is higher in their case.[1] Many of the large holdings, too, showed losses in the years under study when all costs were imputed, suggesting that perhaps even the large holdings do not strictly aim at profit-maximisation (or do not at least succeed in achieving it). A reason that may be suggested (not on the grounds of internal evidence in the FMS however) and which appears to be a reasonable hypothesis is that, for the large land-owner, cultivation happens to be only one source of income. His position as a large landowner in the rural economy with the powers and privileges that accrue, places him in a favourable position to extract incomes from other activities — like money-lending. The lower level of asset formation, irrigation and productive investment in general goes hand-in-hand with the low degree of labour-hire on these holdings. (See 3.18 above). Investment on farm does not appear to be favoured, especially in sparsely irrigated areas. The large holdings in these poorly irrigated areas thus appears to economise on hired labour by concentrating on crops that use less labour. They also have a lower level of irrigation compared to that on smaller farms and therefore produce the sturdier varieties of cereals which can better stand climatic variations. A very small proportion of the area, or none, is devoted to the more lucrative food crops (vegetables, fruits, etc.), possibly, in part, because these require careful management of labour. Also, given the rather austere and low level of consumption which is found to prevail in the regions of poor irrigation, their marketability constitutes an additional problem. Inadequacy of preservation and transport facilities make their production for a distant market and on a large scale additionally risky.

7.8.   The situation appears to change quite significantly in the case of the better irrigated regions like Punjab and U.P. With land better irrigated and risks in cultivation diminished, the area under cash crops (like American cotton in Punjab and sugarcane in U.P.) is seen to be quite high on the large holdings, significantly so in the case of Punjab. The intensity of cultivation shows, however, a significant inverse relation to size of holding, declining sharply on large holdings. This probably explains the significant inverse relation between value productivity per acre and the size of holding found in Punjab despite the predominance of higher value cash crops on large holdings. The relatively lower level of irrigation on these holdings and the relatively higher

1   The scatter of points relating the proportion of hired to total labour and the size of holding indicates that the proportion generally rises with the size of holding.

Table 7.II *Cropping pattern: West Bengal*

Size of holding (acres and crops)	Total labour per acre	Hired labour per acre	Bullock labour per acre	Paid-out cost per acre	Farm business income per acre	Gross revenue per acre	Percentage area under the crop
1	(days) 2	(days) 3	(days) 4	(Rs) 5	(Rs) 6	(Rs) 7	8
0.01–1.25							
Aman paddy	51.1	14.2	13.2	70.5	134.1	204.3	68.09
Aus paddy	75.4	9.6	13.4	44.0	157.3	201.3	1.50
Jute	105.3	n.a.	14.1	103.4	113.2	216.6	18.74
Mesta	88.9	24.4	14.9	79.2	22.6	101.8	2.35
Pulses	25.3	6.7	12.0	38.8	10.2	48.9	6.01
Potato	185.9	79.6	22.6	561.7	226.5	788.2	3.31
1.25–2.50							
Aman paddy	51.0	17.9	15.4	81.4	135.7	217.1	67.18
Aus paddy	38.6	6.8	14.0	60.6	103.6	164.2	3.98
Jute	97.8	n.a.	15.8	94.6	123.0	217.7	14.13
Mesta	74.5	18.6	12.9	73.8	161.9	235.7	4.36
Pulses	19.5	3.4	8.6	33.2	28.6	61.8	7.53
Potato	178.9	73.3	23.9	759.7	123.7	883.4	2.82
2.50–3.75							
Aman paddy	52.9	18.0	16.9	91.7	127.6	219.2	73.76
Aus paddy	66.1	5.7	14.6	47.2	107.9	155.0	1.74
Jute	117.2	n.a.	19.4	116.2	89.8	206.0	13.25
Mesta	89.2	15.5	14.1	73.7	162.3	221.8	2.95
Pulses	38.2	5.6	12.4	49.9	54.6	104.6	6.77
Potato	178.4	59.5	24.4	922.1	−54.7	867.4	1.82

3.75–5.0

Aman paddy	47.1	14.1	13.9	70.5	112.2	182.7	71.64
Aus paddy	44.9	11.9	15.1	65.0	83.9	148.9	3.05
Jute	94.7	n.a.	17.4	108.1	108.7	216.8	13.40
Mesta	75.9	35.6	12.1	103.9	141.7	245.1	2.38
Pulses	21.3	4.8	13.2	38.8	42.0	80.8	7.42
Potato	157.8	35.0	22.3	581.2	163.4	744.6	2.10

5–7.5

Aman paddy	48.6	18.8	13.7	102.3	131.9	234.3	66.11
Aus paddy	56.7	13.7	20.3	108.2	57.3	165.5	5.45
Jute	76.1	–	18.3	118.7	107.8	226.5	12.80
Mesta	74.2	25.0	15.7	128.9	148.3	277.2	4.57
Pulses	24.0	5.2	11.6	40.5	26.0	66.5	9.32
Potato	22.1	76.7	23.5	699.6	228.3	927.9	1.76

7.5–10.0

Aman paddy	43.1	17.3	14.4	90.1	141.4	237.5	77.52
Aus paddy	51.4	5.3	12.3	73.1	114.7	187.8	3.89
Jute	104.9	–	18.5	82.7	159.4	242.1	9.89
Mesta	66.4	9.8	8.7	109.8	211.3	321.0	1.82
Pulses	24.3	6.8	11.0	32.6	36.8	61.4	5.42
Potato	130.3	13.0	26.0	337.2	572.5	909.6	1.45

10.0–15.0

Aman paddy	39.5	28.6	12.6	81.6	90.0	171.6	64.74
Aus paddy	64.1	13.1	13.4	66.7	141.7	208.4	2.21
Jute	71.2	–	13.6	98.9	164.7	263.6	13.41
Mesta	50.1	39.4	9.6	75.8	98.8	174.5	5.92
Pulses	20.5	18.5	11.3	47.1	22.6	76.9	13.17
Potato	145.5	8.0	23.2	238.9	841.4	1080.4	0.55

Table 7.II   *(continued)*

Size of holding (acres and crops)	Total labour per acre	Hired labour per acre	Bullock labour per acre	Paid-out cost per acre	Farm business income per acre	Gross revenue per acre	Percentage area under the crop
1	(days) 2	(days) 3	(days) 4	(Rs) 5	(Rs) 6	(Rs) 7	8
15 and above							
Aman paddy	42.3	26.2	11.9	77.7	119.5	196.2	68.22
Aus paddy	51.5	–	18.0	37.9	127.8	165.3	1.75
Jute	83.3	–	18.1	158.6	65.2	223.8	10.54
Mesta	115.8	24.0	11.3	53.3	261.7	315.0	1.38
Pulses	17.6	4.7	4.2	15.7	33.0	48.7	16.56
Potato	146.3	61.9	25.9	500.9	217.5	718.4	1.55

wage rate in the region[2] which discourages hire of labour, may partly explain the low intensity of cultivation. With new technology inputs like fertilisers, mechanised implements, tubewell irrigation, hybrid seeds etc., this situation may possibly change.

Some observations on cropping patterns

7.9.   With a view to studying the size-group-wise variations in cropping pattern we have recorded for each individual crop and for each size group of holding, labour input, bullock labour, costs actually incurred (i.e. paid-out-cost), as also gross revenue and farm business income, all *per acre*. Alongside we have given also the percentage of area allocated to the crop on that size-class of holdings. (See Tables 7.II to 7.VII). The following brief comments relate to the pattern observed in individual regions.

7.10.   *West Bengal:* The two major crops of the region are paddy (*Aman* and *Aus*) and jute, of which Aman paddy occupies a large area. The proportion of area allocated to the crop is smallest (about 67 per cent) on the very small group (below 1.25 acres) and rises thereafter. It remains high for middle farmers (5 to 10 acres) and falls again to 68 per cent on the large group (above 10 acres). Aman paddy does not absorb as much labour and bullock power as jute; the paid-out cost per acre is also lower, but it brings in a lower gross revenue per acre. Jute absorbs a large amount of human labour per acre. It has a higher paid-out cost per acre relative to other crops but yields a higher gross revenue per acre as well. It is particularly favoured by the very small farms of under 1.25 acres. The proportion allocated to jute falls as the average size increases to rise again in the last two size groups, i.e. for large holdings above 10 acres. Mesta, again a crop absorbing a significant amount of labour and of bullock labour, with a high paid-out cost per acre but yielding a high gross revenue per acre, absorbs a relatively higher proportion of area on small and middle size holdings (up to 7.50 acres). The proportion is lower thereafter. It is not so much favoured on 'very small' holdings possibly because of the rather high hired labour component and high bullock labour requirements per acre. Potatoes, again a very labour-intensive crop requiring also a very high bullock labour input but bringing in a very large gross revenue per acre, are grown on a very small proportion of area, but the proportion declines over size-classes. On the other hand, pulses, a hardier crop requiring much less labour per acre but yielding also less gross revenue per acre, are allocated a much higher proportion of area on large holdings (above 10 acres). This crop occupies 5 to 7 per cent of area on other holdings and about 13 and 17 per cent on the highest two size groups.

7.11.   *Uttar Pradesh:* Sugarcane planted and ratoon are the main cash crops of the region. Sugarcane planted requires a high amount of labour and of bullock input (though not as high as for wheat) and a high paid-out cost per acre but yields the highest gross revenue per acre. It is favoured by the very small (up to 2.5 acre) group. Sugarcane ratoon, which also requires a high amount of labour input but lower bullock labour input per acre and brings in the next highest gross revenue per

2   The average wage rate for 1954—57 was Rs. 2.60 per day. Punjab also shows wider seasonal fluctuations, the peak period rate rising to Rs. 3.50 per day.

Table 7.III Cropping pattern: U.P.

Size of holding (acres) and crops	Total labour per acre (days)	Bullock labour per acre (days)	Paid out costs per acre (Rs.)	Farm business income per acre (Rs.)	Gross revenue per acre (Rs.)	Percentage area under the crop
1	2	3	4	5	6	7
0.0–2.5						
Sugarcane planted	71	12	261	287	547	21.29
Sugarcane ratoon	49	5	104	363	467	29.21
Irrigated wheat	33	19	205	23	234	36.39
Unirrigated wheat	28	13	142	−11	154	
Gram	8	1	60	−27	34	9.85
Paddy	20	8	76	166	242	3.26
2.5–5.0						
Sugarcane planted	85	16	272	170	442	18.97
Sugarcane ratoon	48	8	125	312	436	23.00
Irrigated wheat	39	20	188	39	233	42.00
Unirrigated wheat	30	19	125	−3	132	
Gram	19	7	71	27	98	9.99
Paddy	39	9	93	32	125	5.96
5.0–7.5						
Sugarcane planted	74	14	238	222	308	21.47
Sugarcane ratoon	54	10	128	266	315	22.15
Irrigated wheat	31	21	164	58	566	39.15
Unirrigated wheat	32	20	134	−6	219	
Gram	14	–	50	20	158	11.09
Paddy	47	8	90	64	79	5.54

7.5–10.0

Sugarcane planted	77	16	224	214	508	20.03
Sugarcane ratoon	48	8	112	273	527	21.64
Irrigated wheat	0	16	129	85	99	⎫
Unirrigated wheat	28	17	117	3	169	⎬ 40.67
Gram	16	6	46	16	265	10.89
Paddy	30	7	71	63	146	5.97

10–15

Sugarcane planted	72	15	221	198	558	17.55
Sugarcane ratoon	50	10	117	226	596	18.76
Irrigated wheat	30	17	138	51	138	⎫
Unirrigated wheat	27	17	109	6	120	⎬ 43.41
Gram	12	5	50	15	362	11.40
Paddy	35	9	96	51	283	8.89

15–20

Sugarcane planted	77	17	231	242	469	22.40
Sugarcane ratoon	54	10	111	281	392	17.28
Irrigated wheat	32	17	133	76	215	⎫
Unirrigated wheat	25	14	106	−10	96	⎬ 45.89
Gram	17	9	54	36	90	10.29
Paddy	26	8	85	69	154	4.16

20–25

Sugarcane planted	73	14	216	261	477	22.75
Sugarcane ratoon	35	6	83	246	329	19.16
Irrigated wheat	30	18	128	63	196	⎫
Unirrigated wheat	25	16	100	20	119	⎬ 61.06
Gram	8	5	35	—	35	10.79
Paddy	34	8	99	13	112	6.27

Table 7.III   *(continued)*

Size of holding (acres) and crops	Total labour per acre (days)	Bullock labour per acre (days)	Paid out costs per acre (Rs.)	Farm business income per acre (Rs.)	Gross revenue per acre (Rs.)	Percentage area under the crop
1	2	3	4	5	6	7
25 and above						
Sugarcane planted	59	15	207	259	469	26.91
Sugarcane ratoon	38	6	100	268	369	18.11
Irrigated wheat	27	16	125	65	195	} 40.83
Unirrigated wheat	25	14	94	30	113	
Gram	12	5	42	–	50	10.31
Paddy	46	13	103	110	222	5.83

72

acre as compared to sugarcane planted, is even more favoured by this group of very small farmers (29 per cent area devoted to it compared with 21 per cent under sugarcane). The proportion of area devoted to sugarcane ratoon falls in the middle groups (5 to 10 acres) and rises slightly on large holdings (above 10 acres). Wheat, which requires comparatively less labour per acre and more bullock labour than sugarcane but brings in much less gross revenue per acre, rises generally with the size of holdings, a relatively greater proportion of area being devoted to it in the 10–20 acre group; the proportion falls somewhat on the large holdings above 20 acres where sugarcane reasserts its importance. Paddy, which requires much lower labour input than sugarcane, is a relatively minor crop and the area devoted to it generally increases with the size of holding. Gram, another of the relatively minor crops, does not show much variation in the proportion of area devoted to it over the different size-classes of holdings, possibly because it is grown more for self-consumption.

7.12.   *Punjab:* Wheat (irrigated and unirrigated) and cotton (American and *Desi*) are the main crops in the region. We find that, even on very small holdings below 5 acres, American cotton and *Desi* cotton play an important part. The percentage area allocated to cotton declines above this group up to the 20 acre group (i.e. small and middle groups) after which it rises again on the large holdings. In the very large holdings of above 50 acres it occupies about 64 per cent of area. American cotton absorbs a higher level of labour input per acre, a little less bullock labour and paid-out cost per acre as compared to irrigated wheat, and brings in a high gross revenue per acre. *Desi* cotton, while absorbing somewhat less bullock labour input and paid-out costs per acre than American cotton, brings in a lower gross revenue per acre. It also occupies a rather small percentage of area as compared to American cotton on all holdings. Irrigated wheat and irrigated wheat gram absorb a high level of labour input as well as bullock labour, but the gross revenue per acre is higher for wheat. The area allocated to wheat and irrigated wheat gram remains around 26 and 36 per cent respectively up to 10 acres and then shows a continuous decline. While in the 10–50 acre group unirrigated wheat-gram gains relative importance at the cost of irrigated wheat-gram and cotton, in the largest group of above 55 acres it is American cotton that gains at the cost of all others. The varying importance of irrigated wheat-gram possibly reflects the levels of irrigation on the holdings. It is a crop which absorbs much less material inputs, producing lower revenue per acre as well.

7.13.   *Madras:* Complete information for the individual crops was not available except for paddy, cotton and *cholam.* Table 7.V gives the percentage distribution of area between different crops. Paddy requires a very large amount of human labour and bullock labour per acre. The paid-out cost per acre is also very high, and it requires an adequate water-supply. Although it yields a high gross revenue per acre, the very small holdings (below 2.5 acres) favour cotton and groundnuts (the two important cash crops), possibly because of the excessively high cost and bullock labour requirements of paddy. Cotton, while yielding a high enough gross revenue per acre (more than *cholam*), requires less bullock labour per acre. On the small farms (2.5 to 5 acres) paddy and *ragi* gain in importance while groundnuts and cotton decline. The middle group (5 to 15 acres) produces a more even mix of crops, while

Table 7.IV Cropping pattern: Punjab

Size of holding (acres)	Total labour per acre (days)	Hired labour per acre (days)	Bullock labour per acre (days)	Paid-out costs per acre (Rs.)	Farm business income per acre (Rs.)	Gross revenue per acre (Rs.)	Percentage area under the crop
0–5							
Irrigated wheat	29.3	4.5	25.6	69.2	30.9	159.1	25.73
Irrigated wheat-gram	21.7	2.3	19.3	69.4	72.6	125.7	36.96
Unirrigated wheat-gram	17.2	2.9	15.6	58.9	41.3	100.3	8.39
American cotton	31.0	4.4	14.8	51.5	86.6	131.0	22.76
Desi cotton	26.0	2.8	16.1	45.9	50.9	91.9	6.16
5–10							
Irrigated wheat	25.3	2.3	26.2	70.5	68.4	139.3	27.79
Irrigated wheat-gram	21.9	2.6	19.6	62.1	64.4	112.7	35.37
Unirrigated wheat-gram	15.8	1.7	16.4	40.2	38.0	85.8	8.53
American cotton	33.3	6.1	19.3	51.7	90.2	165.0	24.57
Desi cotton	29.0	2.8	15.2	40.2	38.9	91.4	3.73
10–20							
Irrigated wheat	28.8	4.7	27.3	77.2	98.5	173.2	24.90
Irrigated wheat-gram	20.2	3.9	19.0	61.2	74.8	122.7	27.80
Unirrigated wheat-gram	26.2	2.2	14.8	48.4	52.3	88.8	20.23
American cotton	31.5	8.4	17.4	52.1	101.9	150.0	22.96
Desi cotton	34.2	6.3	15.0	52.9	77.6	132.3	4.11

20–50

Irrigated wheat	27.3	6.4	24.3	79.2	100.8	177.7	24.79
Irrigated wheat-gram	19.6	5.2	18.7	63.8	67.8	122.7	22.06
Unirrigated wheat-gram	13.8	3.4	13.1	44.5	55.5	85.1	22.35
American cotton	38.0	13.3	16.8	73.1	143.3	231.0	26.75
Desi cotton	36.0	9.7	14.3	57.6	96.1	152.8	4.05

50 and above

Irrigated wheat	22.3	14.2	19.0	92.6	132.1	213.8	16.83
Irrigated wheat-gram	15.0	5.8	14.4	60.0	57.4	106.0	10.92
Unirrigated wheat-gram	12.3	6.3	15.2	60.2	34.5	93.0	7.57
American cotton	28.4	19.6	14.7	72.6	127.5	320.0	62.77
Desi cotton	25.6	13.3	14.8	66.6	83.4	140.0	1.91

on the large holdings (above 15 acres) paddy (which absorbs a very large amount of labour) declines considerably in importance, as also does cotton, while the sturdier crops, *ragi* and *cumbu,* occupy a greater proportion of area.

7.14.   *Bombay:* Ahmednagar and Nasik have somewhat different cropping patterns. *Bajri* and *jowar* predominate, with wheat and gram as minor crops in Ahmednagar, while *bajri* and wheat dominate the pattern in Nasik, with gram receiving a somewhat higher allocation than in Ahmednagar, (see Table 7.VI). The non-food crops (which are not important in either district) receive the highest percentage allocation on the very small farms (below 5 acres), declining in importance on the small farms (5 to 10 acres), increasing somewhat on middle farms (10 to 20 acres), only to decline again on the large (above 20 acres). *Jowar* and *bajri* are somewhat comparable crops as far as labour and bullock input per acre are concerned. *Bajri* yields a relatively higher gross revenue per acre but requires a better water supply. With a somewhat higher level of irrigation on smaller holdings, this crop occupies a larger proportion of area on these holdings in Ahmednagar. The distribution of area between *bajri* and *jowar* appears to be dictated by climatic factors (see 5.12). In Nasik, wheat, which is a relatively labour intensive crop, is favoured on very small holdings (below 5 acres) while *bajri* appears to partly displace it on the very large holdings (above 50 acres). In Nasik, vegetables (included in 'other crops') are grown predominantly on small and middle holdings (5 to 20 acres).

7.15.   *Madhya Pradesh:* Crop-wise data on inputs are not available for Madhya Pradesh, but Table 7.VII gives the cropping pattern for unirrigated areas according to the size of holding. The irrigated area forms a very minor proportion and is mostly devoted to the production of fruits and vegetables. It may be noticed that on the very small (below 5 acres) size group the proportion of area under cereals is less and that under cash crops (oilseeds, cotton) is more than on other holdings. Commenting on this the Report remarks (1955–56, p. 23) 'In almost all the size-groups of holding about half of the area is under food crops and of the remaining about 80 percent under cotton. The only exception being the smallest size-group where the area under food crops is less than even half the area. The above crop pattern leads one to think that the subsistence needs of a farmer in this tract play a little part in determining the crop pattern. If that would have been the fact more percentage area under food crops is expected in smalller holdings than in bigger ones. If anything is borne out by this data, it is contrary to this.' It is evident from our discussion that while the very small farmers do not directly grow the subsistence crops, their production activity is geared to providing subsistence for which they need to raise cash crops.

7.16.   We have in this section indicated how the resource position of the cultivator, as well as the nature and the extent of his involvement in the markets, determines for him the objectives of production activity and influences the use of inputs as well as his cropping pattern.

Table 7.V   *Cropping pattern: Madras [both districts combined]*

Size-group (acres)	Proportion of area under:							
	Paddy	Cholam	Ragi	Cumbu	Other crops	Total of food crops	Cotton	Groundnut
0.0–2.5	10.0	16.7	18.1	7.6	16.9	69.3	19.6	11.1
2.5–5.0	16.8	9.2	20.3	9.0	22.6	77.9	12.2	9.9
5.0–7.5	13.7	15.0	14.5	10.6	21.7	75.5	10.7	13.8
7.5–10.0	18.3	13.0	18.6	7.8	24.6	82.3	11.4	6.3
10.0–15.0	11.5	19.2	13.4	13.6	24.7	82.4	9.1	8.5
15.0–20.0	2.4	20.8	8.9	16.4	23.1	71.6	16.0	12.4
20.0–25.0	7.4	14.1	6.0	23.8	37.0	88.3	5.8	5.9
25.0 & above	4.3	10.5	25.2	11.4	36.8	88.2	3.1	8.7

77

Table 7.VIA Cropping pattern: Bombay – Ahmednagar

Size of holding (acres) and crops	Total labour days per acre	Bullock labour days per acre	Paid-out costs per acre (Rs.)	Farm business income per acre (Rs.)	Gross revenue per acre (Rs.)	Percentage area under the crop[a]
1	2	3	4	5	6	7
0–5						
Dry jowar	21.9	15.6	34.9	0.8	34.8	} 29.03
Irrigated jowar	48.3	33.4	45.6	59.2	118.7	
Dry wheat	15.0	23.6	45.5	49.4	78.6	} 6.23
Irrigated wheat	44.0	49.4	72.1	56.6	131.6	
Dry gram	12.3	4.4	17.1	−2.8	12.6	} 3.23
Irrigated gram	7.5	3.7	35.5	−31.2	12.4	
Dry bajri	25.6	18.4	29.4	24.3	74.2	38.71
5–10						
Dry jowar	13.3	11.5	11.3	19.1	30.7	} 41.97
Irrigated jowar	28.7	32.7	37.9	62.4	101.5	
Dry wheat	12.5	14.9	34.6	15.4	38.3	} 7.41
Irrigated wheat	47.7	53.4	70.6	66.7	138.9	
Dry gram	11.9	6.7	16.8	−1.9	26.7	} 2.23
Irrigated gram	20.8	23.3	27.9	−8.5	81.1	
Dry bajri	21.0	18.1	36.0	16.3	50.0	32.10
10–15						
Dry jowar	12.1	9.7	12.0	16.8	28.8	} 47.41
Irrigated jowar	34.4	33.7	42.7	40.1	93.1	
Dry wheat	13.9	18.7	31.4	18.6	50.6	} 3.40
Irrigated wheat	47.8	50.5	79.0	49.3	136.0	
Dry gram	14.5	12.6	17.9	17.3	28.4	} 3.45
Irrigated gram	26.5	28.6	39.2	1.4	32.5	
Dry bajri	17.1	12.8	22.2	13.2	40.8	26.72

15—20						
Dry jowar	11.1	11.4	15.0	28.4	44.8	} 44.9
Irrigated jowar	35.1	34.7	29.0	81.7	114.4	
Dry wheat	14.6	17.8	48.6	50.9	70.2	} 3.00
Irrigated wheat	41.7	40.0	46.0	42.4	91.9	
Dry gram	12.6	11.8	20.2	41.3	53.8	} 1.80
Irrigated gram	29.8	26.0	30.3	40.8	72.1	
Dry bajri	16.3	11.9	15.8	17.2	37.4	} 30.54
20—25						
Dry jowar	9.0	10.0	12.2	12.0	23.8	} 58.29
Irrigated jowar	40.6	40.6	49.4	34.0	107.7	
Dry wheat	34.6	29.8	26.5	21.3	64.7	} 2.70
Irrigated wheat	53.7	64.8	75.1	36.0	109.5	
Dry gram	9.0	4.8	12.4	25.3	49.6	} 2.24
Irrigated gram	22.6	20.8	33.8	31.4	77.7	
Dry bajri	17.8	14.3	17.5	13.2	25.1	} 21.97
25—30						
Dry jowar	8.8	9.5	14.8	15.6	30.0	} 48.63
Irrigated jowar	31.0	38.3	33.8	63.5	109.1	
Dry wheat	11.4	8.8	28.5	−20.7	17.3	} 2.40
Irrigated wheat	43.8	60.1	75.5	59.7	132.5	
Dry gram	8.7	7.3	15.5	6.8	26.8	} 3.92
Irrigated gram	15.6	16.3	27.6	17.0	50.9	
Dry bajri	16.1	13.5	18.5	14.6	22.4	} 30.5
30—50						
Dry jowar	11.0	13.9	15.2	14.5	29.2	} 42.41
Irrigated jowar	31.7	31.7	28.7	61.5	100.4	
Dry wheat	17.4	22.5	30.9	24.6	61.1	} 4.60
Irrigated wheat	28.7	31.5	50.8	27.9	77.9	
Dry gram	9.2	8.1	18.6	16.5	22.3	} 4.33
Irrigated gram	24.2	24.6	35.2	3.3	43.9	
Dry bajri	15.8	12.5	18.3	20.1	34.0	} 30.65

Table 7.VIA (continued)

Size of holding (acres) and crops	Total labour days per acre	Bullock labour days per acre	Paid-out costs per acre (Rs.)	Farm business income per acre (Rs.)	Gross revenue per acre (Rs.)	Percentage area under the crop
1	2	3	4	5	6	7
50 and above						
Dry *jowar*	8.7	8.8	12.0	14.5	27.5	} 46.46
Irrigated *jowar*	32.7	19.2	34.6	62.1	100.9	
Dry wheat	18.1	22.3	22.0	22.3	57.5	} 2.90
Irrigated wheat	42.2	42.2	78.6	85.8	164.1	
Dry gram	11.8	10.2	23.3	25.3	35.3	} 2.50
Irrigated gram	23.1	34.5	32.2	50.8	98.4	
Dry *bajri*	9.1	8.8	8.3	11.0	20.8	28.13

ᵃ Area under a crop includes the dry and the irrigated

Table 7.VIB *Cropping pattern: Bombay – Nasik*

Size of holding (acres) and crops	Total labour days per acre	Bullock labour days per acre	Paid-out costs per acre (Rs.)	Farm business income per acre (Rs.)	Gross revenue per acre (Rs.)	Percentage area under the crop
1	2	3	4	5	6	7
0–5						
Dry wheat	15.3	24.6	45.4	−1.8	43.5	} 22.32
Irrigated wheat	51.2	60.8	77.5	−35.1	95.0	
Dry gram	13.8	10.6	23.7	11.0	36.9	} 8.33
Irrigated gram	59.6	51.3	62.0	−6.1	54.0	
Dry bajri	25.6	18.4	29.4	38.9	70.6	41.66
5–10						
Dry wheat	16.3	21.7	36.6	14.1	53.0	} 21.94
Irrigated wheat	50.6	68.8	89.0	21.8	121.1	
Dry gram	13.4	10.1	23.1	−9.3	28.6	} 8.24
Irrigated gram	24.4	35.9	42.5	5.8	51.6	
Dry bajri	21.0	18.1	36.0	38.1	62.3	43.53
10–15						
Dry wheat	13.8	18.3	40.1	0.8	39.2	} 15.65
Irrigated wheat	65.7	74.6	99.8	52.7	150.2	
Dry gram	12.6	11.9	27.4	1.8	29.2	} 6.09
Irrigated gram	34.0	38.0	45.2	−2.1	40.9	
Dry bajri	17.1	12.8	22.2	18.2	40.7	49.56
15–20						
Dry wheat	12.5	19.5	25.2	17.8	43.2	} 13.84
Irrigated wheat	62.5	79.1	115.7	14.6	131.9	
Dry gram	19.2	15.5	24.1	16.8	41.4	} 4.40
Irrigated gram	27.8	39.0	50.4	2.7	56.4	
Dry bajri	16.3	11.9	15.8	19.0	35.3	53.45

Table 7.VIB (continued)

Size of holding (acres) and crops	Total labour days per acre	Bullock labour days per acre	Paid-out costs per acre (Rs.)	Farm business income per acre (Rs.)	Gross revenue per acre (Rs.)	Percentage area under the crop
1	2	3	4	5	6	7
20–25						
Dry wheat	12.9	17.3	30.9	8.6	42.3	} 11.51
Irrigated wheat	71.8	87.0	109.5	25.3	141.5	}
Dry gram	16.3	13.3	19.3	12.9	33.1	5.61
Irrigated gram	27.2	37.8	36.4	−2.4	31.7	
Dry bajri	17.8	14.3	17.5	30.7	48.2	41.83
25–30						
Dry wheat	13.6	19.2	25.1	22.7	48.8	} 11.49
Irrigated wheat	56.5	74.1	97.8	33.2	144.8	}
Dry gram	19.8	18.5	23.6	8.1	35.9	} 5.15
Irrigated gram	25.7	33.2	30.8	21.0	52.6	}
Dry bajri	16.1	13.5	18.5	30.0	58.2	38.09
30–50						
Dry wheat	14.6	21.0	37.3	2.0	39.3	} 11.08
Irrigated wheat	48.1	67.2	64.7	36.5	103.6	}
Dry gram	14.8	15.1	28.0	7.4	37.3	} 3.69
Irrigated gram	36.8	40.4	48.6	0.5	51.4	}
Dry bajri	15.8	12.5	18.3	15.0	33.4	47.69
50 and above						
Dry wheat	11.8	20.6	31.4	8.4	38.9	} 9.51
Irrigated wheat	26.7	37.1	48.8	−12.9	51.0	}
Dry gram	17.0	17.0	35.6	1.5	29.2	} 3.77
Irrigated gram	26.5	35.6	48.2	12.9	63.2	}
Dry bajri	9.1	8.8	8.3	10.8	24.5	60.50

Table 7.VII Cropping pattern for unirrigated area according to size of holding: Madhya Pradesh (1956–57)[a]

| Size of holding (acres) | Percentage of area under: | | | | | | | |
	Cereals	Pulses	Total food crops	Fibres – mainly cotton	Oil seeds	Other cash crops	Total cash crops
0–5	29.61	17.08	46.69	41.56	7.88	3.87	53.31
5–10	33.30	17.57	50.87	40.27	6.17	2.69	49.13
10–15	37.70	18.92	56.62	30.06	9.83	3.49	43.38
15–20	36.48	17.92	54.40	36.21	7.99	1.40	45.60
20–30	33.86	16.72	52.58	41.00	4.90	1.52	47.42
30–40	35.45	21.36	56.81	34.44	7.31	1.44	43.19
40–50	41.74	19.35	61.10	32.51	4.63	1.76	38.90
50 and above	32.12	16.45	48.58	44.58	5.79	1.05	51.42

a   The proportion of area irrigated to total cultivated area is negligible in the region. On the irrigated land mainly fruits and vegetables are grown.

8
Summing up

8.1.   In this Occasional Paper we have analysed some aspects of production conditions in Indian agriculture on the basis of the published *Studies in the Economics of Farm Management*. Given the nature of the data contained therein, the focus has inevitably been on the technological relations between inputs and outputs especially in relation to size of holdings. Most published research based on FMS has likewise concentrated on such relations. The present paper, while sharing this bias, attempts to move away from the competitive premises which have explicitly or implicitly provided the analytical basis for such studies. We have argued, for example, that the usual exercises comparing factor prices with estimated marginal productivities of factors ignore the specific characteristics of agrarian market relations. In the introductory section we began by discussing some specific characteristic features of production relations in agriculture which rule out the competitive premises.

8.2.   In Chapter 2 we took up the familiar debate on the 'inverse relation' between yield per acre and size of holding. Arguing from purely technological relations, we concluded that this inverse relation may be attributed to differences in intensity of cultivation and in cropping patterns — the smaller holdings generally cultivating land more intensively and/or producing crops of greater value per acre. This conclusion is by no means original or striking although in the current literature on the subject, cropping pattern has not received much attention. Our emphasis on these two factors, especially cropping pattern, is derived partly from a recurrent finding that a technical relation between input use (or productivity) and size of holding which appears to find support at the level of total crop production activity, fails to do so for individual crops. Intensity of cultivation and cropping pattern, we suggest, are in turn influenced by particular characteristics of markets (for both inputs and outputs), by the resource position of the individual operator and by the nature and extent of his involvement in these markets. While all three features are interrelated, the complexity of their interaction cannot be fully brought out given the limited informational basis of the FMS. Nevertheless, primarily as a suggestive and indicative effort, in subsequent sections (Chapters 3 and 4) we have attempted to analyse how the use of human labour, bullock labour and other inputs are influenced by such factors.

8.3.   In Chapter 3 we discussed, among other topics, the question why employment *on farm* and *off farm* are not independent choices for the operator and how the opportunity to take outside employment depends partly upon the size of holding. We also noted how the distribution of work among different categories of workers may be determined by extra-economic factors (i.e. apart from wages). More generally, we discussed the reasons why family labour and hired labour may not be treated either as perfectly substitutive or as exclusive categories. We argued thence that the usual exercises which judge the efficiency of labour use on the basis of a comparison of marginal productivity of labour (estimated from a fitted production function) with wages, are out of place. First, there are difficulties with the notion of the diminishing marginal productivity of labour itself; given the nature of the intertemporal distribution of labour inputs, the productivity of the preceding labour inputs depends crucially upon the application of the required quantities of labour at harvest time. Secondly, there are difficulties in interpreting the wage rate as the opportunity cost of labour given the characteristics of the labour market.

8.4.   In Chapter 4 we noted the significance attached to the ownership of bullocks in a rural society and discussed how the indivisibility of this asset, the seasonality in its use, the availability of irrigational facilities, etc., influence its use on holdings. In Chapter 5 while analysing the availability and effects of irrigation observed on different holding-sizes, we again referred to the broader set of forces that are relevant to the problem: namely, the different objectives which different producers pursue (or can be said to pursue) given their resource position, and how these objectives influence the distribution and utilisation of irrigational facilities. For example, we suggested that the big landlord may prefer to parcel out the irrigated land into small plots to petty tenants. This may be *one* of the reasons why smaller operational holdings are generally better irrigated. Again, the smaller irrigated holdings are cultivated at a level of intensity beyond the point of maximum *net* return; this is possibly due to the fact that the petty cultivators are interested in *gross* rather than *net* output.

8.5.   The complex character of market relations emerges somewhat more sharply when we turn to tenurial conditions and the cropping pattern in Chapters 6 and 7 respectively. The information on tenurial conditions contained in the published FMS is extremely scanty and partial so that our discussion remains highly cursory and tentative. Within these limitations, we have suggested a few hypotheses concerning the way in which the type of tenancy (i.e. fixed-rent or share-cropping) and the 'level of tenancy' (i.e. percentage area of the farm leased-in) affect the intensity of cultivation, input costs, the cropping pattern etc. There are marked interregional variations so that generalizations, especially based on such poor information, are hazardous. In Chapter 7 dealing with cropping patterns, we tried to classify the cultivators into four categories — namely, 'very small', 'small', 'middle' and 'large'. This classification is based on the nature of their market involvement which is in turn determined by their initial resource position. We discussed the factors influencing the crop pattern of each of these groups of farmers. For example, we noted that the very small farmers who are compulsively involved in markets tend to devote a higher proportion of their area to cash crops while the small farmers who can to some extent protect themselves from markets tend to produce predominantly subsistence crops. The middle cultivators, who can secure some surplus over subsistence, appear to produce a variety of crops including crops of high value requiring careful management (like vegetables), while big farmers have a different pattern in sparsely irrigated areas as compared with the better irrigated areas like Punjab and U.P. In the former, they concentrate on the sturdier but low-valued crops, while in the latter they devote a considerable proportion of their area to high-value cash crops.

8.6.   The purpose of this Occasional Paper is limited to evolving a framework with which to *describe* production conditions rather than predicting the shape of the future or deducing policy conclusions. Before attempting prediction or the drawing out of prescriptive inferences, it is necessary to devise suitable categories in terms of which the interrelations within the economy may be worked out. It appears to us that a meaningful analysis of a changing agrarian economy could be carried out by studying the process of its commercialization. This process can itself be described in terms of the extent and nature of the market involvement of different groups of peasantry, the interlocked character of markets, and the way in which the power relations in the rural economy are reflected in, and are influenced by, market relations.

Appendix A

A note on the FMS:
design of the enquiry and concepts

The Farm Management investigations were launched by the Directorate of Economics and Statistics and the Research Programmes Committee in 1954-55 in five typical regions (Punjab, West Bengal, Bombay, Uttar Pradesh, Madras) and then extended to Madhya Pradesh in 1955-56. Two contiguous districts were selected in each as representing its typical soil crop complex. (Amritsar and Ferozpur in Punjab; Hooghly and 24 Paraganas in West Bengal; Ahmednagar and Nasik in Bombay; Meerut and Muzaffarnagar in U.P.; Coimbatore and Salem in Madras; and Akola and Amraoti in Madhya Pradesh, now in Maharashtra). The investigation was carried over three years, 1954-55, 1955-56, and 1956-57, except for Madhya Pradesh where it covered only the last two.

The enquiry adopted a multi-stage stratified random sampling with villages as the primary unit and the holding as the ultimate unit. Two alternative methods of investigation were adopted, called the 'Cost Accounting Method' and the 'Survey Method'. In each state two contiguous districts were first selected representing the typical soil-complex of the region. Each district was subdivided into two fairly homogeneous zones on the basis of agricultural and climatic conditions, and the villages were then selected at random with probability proportional to the cultivating population. The ultimate unit of the enquiry was the 'operational holding' comprising all the land cultivated by the selected farmer irrespective of location or ownership. The selection of holdings was arrived at after ranking the holdings in each village in ascending (or descending) order according to their size. The total number of holdings were then divided into five size groups, each containing an equal number of holdings. From each group, holdings were selected with equal probability, two under the cost accounting method and four under the survey method. Thus for each region, 200 holdings were selected under the Cost Accounting Method and 400 holdings under the Survey Method.

Information was collected on the basis of two schedules — 'village forms' and 'holding forms'. The former provided general information concerning the village area, population, livestock, soil-types, climatic conditions, land utilisation, demographic characteristics etc. These were common to both the 'Cost Accounting' and the 'Survey' methods. The two methods differed in the 'Holding' forms which enquired into operation costs, maintenance of livestock, purchase and sale of products etc. Although the schedules were similar under the two methods they covered different periods of reference. Data were recorded intensively on a day-to-day basis

87

during the enquiry period in the Cost Accounting Method, while in the Survey method they referred to the entire period (usually two to three months) intervening between the periodic visits of the investigator. The analysis of findings by the two methods indicated that the Cost Accounting Method provided more reliable information although in many cases the results were not too divergent. We have used the Cost Accounting data in our study here.

The Reports furnish detailed data concerning costs incurred in cash or in kind — of production activities relating to major individual crops as well as total crop production. These are furnished according to size-groups of operational holding. Data on utilisation of family and hired labour (in physical and money units), owned and hired bullock labour (in days and money units), other current inputs like seeds etc., overhead charges paid in the form of land revenue, rents, irrigation and other cesses, depreciation and interest charges on capital, are presented individually for major crops and for total crop production by size-groups of holdings. In some reports a few particulars about irrigational facilities and tenurial conditions are included.

In analysing costs and returns, four different cost concepts have been used. 'Cost A_1' (called Cost A in some reports) is the cash and kind expenses actually incurred assuming that the holding is operated by an owner-operator; i.e., it comprises cash and kind expenditures incurred in hiring human labour, for the purchase of seeds, manures and other inputs, for payment of land revenue and irrigation and other cesses, depreciation charges on fixed assets and interest on crop loans, if any. 'Cost A_2' is the cost of farming operations to a *tenant operator* and is arrived at by adding to Cost A_1 the rent paid out by the tenant-operator who leases-in the land. (It is evident that to the *owner-cultivator* the two costs coincide). 'Cost B', adds to Cost A_1, apart from rents actually paid on leased-in land, imputed rent on owned land and imputed interest on owned capital (implements and buildings). 'Cost C' which is the most comprehensive of the cost concepts adds to Cost B the imputed value of labour of the farm operator and his family. The interpretation of the net returns computed on the basis of these various cost concepts should be evident: an owner operator would be concerned with gross income minus cost A_1 (and a tenant operator with gross income minus cost A_2) if he were guided by the return to his expenses actually incurred. This, called in the Surveys 'Farm Business Income', constitutes returns to the farm operator's and his family's labour together with that on owned capital and on owned land. Gross Income minus Cost B is called in the reports 'Family Labour Income' in so far as it is the return to the farm operator's and his family's labour. Profit or loss is defined as gross income minus Cost C. In a fully monetized and capitalist economy it is this last concept of return as net income that would be relevant. In our study we have used at places Cost A_2 (costs actually paid out) and cost C (total cost of inputs), but not cost A or cost B.

1.   *Basis of evaluation:*

The following bases for evaluation of inputs and outputs have been generally used in the FMS:

88

Farm land:

Evaluated according to the local price prevailing for the type of land.

Small implements and equipment:

Valued at current market prices. Annual replacements are treated as expenses.

Purchased livestock:

Evaluated at the original purchase price plus appreciation or minus depreciation. Appreciation is allowed up to 3 years; no depreciation is allowed up to five years and then computed at 20% by the straight line method.

Farm based livestock:

Valued at market prices.

Purchased farm supplies:

Valued at purchase price plus transport, if incurred.

Farm produce and crops:

Valued at prices prevailing at harvest time.

Farmyard manures:

Valued at local market prices. Production of farmyard manure is estimated at the rate of 4 tons per adult animal per month.

Seed:

Purchased seed is valued at actual cost and home grown seed at the prevailing market rate at sowing time.

Bullock labour:

Valued at the prevailing rate for hire.

Livestock maintenance cost:

Home grown fodder is valued at harvest price, purchased seed at the cost price; costs include veterinary charges, upkeep and depreciation.

Depreciation of machinery and implements:

Calculated by the straight line method.

Depreciation of farm buildings:

Depreciation is allowed at 2% for *pucca* buildings and 5% for *kuccha* buildings applying the straight line method.

Allocation of tax and rent among crops:

This is done according to area under different crops. The portion of the crop accruing to the landlord as his share on the leased land is evaluated at harvest price.

Interest on owned capital:

Charged at 3% per annum. Apportionment between different crops is done in proportion of their value.

2.   *Definition of terms*

Size of farm:

includes net cultivated area and current fallows irrespective of ownership.

Net cropped area:

represents farm area *minus* the area of double cropped land.

Gross cropped area:

total area under all crops grown during the year.

Earner:

male member, above 14 years of age, working full time on the farm.

Capital:

investment includes all the real estate held by the farm; namely land, all types of buildings, wells, implements and tools, livestock and other assets. Value of owned but not of leased land is included.

Inputs:

includes human labour, bullock labour, seed, manure, irrigation charges, depreciation of implements, interest on capital, rent and other charges, if any.

Output:

value of the crop produced (value of by-products included only in a few reports).

Operation cost:

includes cost of human labour, bullock labour, seed, manure and irrigation charges.

Overhead cost:

includes interest on capital, depreciation of implements and rent for owned and unowned land.

Appendix B

Land use and productivity

1. *Yield per acre and average size of holding*

We fitted the following functional relation (by the method of ordinary least squares) between yield per acre and the average size of holding for total crop production activity as well as for individual crops:

$$\log Y = \log a + \alpha \log X$$

where Y = yield per (net) acre; yield being defined as gross value of output in the case of total crop activity and as physical quantum of output in the case of individual crops.

and X = average size of operational holding for the relevant size-group.

The estimated parameters and the related statistics, for each state and year, for total crop production are given below in Table B.I. We note that there is generally an inverse relation between the yield per acre and average size of holding. It is statistically significant (at the 5 per cent level) in all the three years for Punjab and not significant for either year for Madhya Pradesh. In other regions, while the relation is statistically significant for one year, it is not so for another.

The same relation was fitted to the following individual crops: irrigated wheat, irrigated wheat-gram, unirrigated wheat-gram, American cotton, Desi cotton in Punjab; *Aman* paddy, *Aus* paddy, jute, mesta, potato and pulses in West Bengal; *Rabi jowar*, irrigated *jowar*, dry wheat, irrigated wheat, dry *bajri*, irrigated *bajri*, dry gram and irrigated gram in Bombay; Paddy Season I, paddy season II, paddy season III, irrigated *cholam* and irrigated cotton in Madras; sugarcane planted, sugarcane ratoon, irrigated wheat, unirrigated wheat, paddy and gram in U.P. In order to save space, we have given in Table B.II the results of the tests carried out only for those cases where the fit was statistically significant at the 10 per cent level. Where the relation was found to be statistically not significant even at the 10 per cent level, we have indicated only the sign of the correlation coefficient (see Table B.III).

It may be noted from Table B.II that the relation between yield per acre and the size of holding turns out to be significant in only a few cases and, of those, it is positive for some and negative for others. Also, for the same crop, it turns out to be significant in some years and not so in others.

Table B.I   *Yield per acre related to size of holding: all crop production*

Region	Year	Constant term	α	Standard error	R^2	F
Punjab	1954-55	2.08	−0.02	0.005	0.79	11.69[b]
	1955-56	1.96	−0.11	0.049	0.83	11.04[b]
	1956-57	2.48	−0.20	0.017	0.96	84.18[a]
West Bengal						
Hooghly	1954-55	2.48	−0.13	0.050	0.55	7.14[b]
24 Paraganas	1954-55	2.40	−0.23	0.145	0.30	2.56
Hooghly	1955-56	2.32	−0.11	0.027	0.72	15.71[a]
24 Paraganas	1955-56	2.31	−0.13	0.057	0.46	5.04[c]
Hooghly	1956-57	2.49	−0.07	0.076	0.12	0.77
24 Paraganas	1956-57	2.35	−0.02	0.066	0.17	0.11
Bombay						
Ahmednagar	1954-55	1.89	−0.30	0.074	0.72	16.28[a]
Nasik	1954-55	2.13	−0.41	0.110	0.71	14.15[a]
Ahmednagar	1955-56	2.02	−0.22	0.166	0.23	1.75
Nasik	1955-56	2.22	−0.31	0.081	0.50	14.69[a]
Ahmednagar	1956-57	2.28	−0.32	0.164	0.41	4.05[c]
Nasik	1956-57	2.28	−0.35	0.089	0.74	16.82[a]
Madras						
	1954-55	2.27	−0.35	0.191	0.36	3.36
	1955-56	2.42	−0.41	0.091	0.75	20.39[a]
	1956-57	2.68	−0.47	0.104	0.75	20.59[a]
U.P.						
	1954-55	2.57	−0.13	0.040	0.75	10.43[b]
	1955-56	2.51	−0.12	0.079	0.43	2.26
	1956-57	2.88	−0.21	0.059	0.67	12.17[a]
M.P.						
Akola	1955-56	2.14	−0.11	0.057	0.38	3.71
Amraoti	1956-57	2.18	−0.08	0.065	0.21	1.50
Akola	1955-56	1.83	−0.02	0.059	0.03	0.15
Amraoti	1956-57	1.69	0.14	0.029	0.02	2.10

Note: [a] denotes significance at 1 per cent level
[b] denotes significance at 5 per cent level
[c] denotes significance at 10 per cent level

We have tabulated below (in Table B.III) individual crops according to the sign that the correlation coefficient bears in each case though it is statistically not significant. It can be noticed that there are as many, if not more, cases of a positive correlation as of a negative one. Moreover, the same crop comes up with a positive correlation in one year and a negative one in another.

In the case of individual crops we also studied the relation between yield per acre and cropped area. We failed to find any systematic relation between the two. Furthermore, even when there appeared to be a significant relation between yield per acre and the average size of holding, that between yield per acre and cropped area turned out to be not significant. We have not presented the statistical results here as they do not appear to be of much interest.

Table B.II *Yield per acre and size of holding: individual crops*

Region/crop	Year	Constant term	α	Standard error	R^2	F
Punjab						
Wheat irrigated	1955-56	0.74	0.20	0.069	0.75	11.04[b]
	1956-57	2.14	0.17	0.028	0.83	14.92[b]
Wheat-gram irrigated	1955-56	2.36	−0.02	0.09	0.74	9.34[c]
American cotton	1954-55	2.06	0.12	0.039	0.76	9.58[c]
	1955-56	2.04	0.12	0.049	0.79	12.42[b]
Desi cotton	1954-55	0.43	0.28	0.068	0.71	16.51[b]
West Bengal						
Aman paddy Hooghly	1956-57	1.20	0.12	0.037	0.61	9.66[b]
Aus paddy Hooghly	1955-56	0.64	0.47	0.053	0.96	77.77[a]
Pulses: Hooghly	1955-56	0.38	0.23	0.082	0.55	8.14[b]
Mesta: Hooghly	1956-57	0.89	0.18	0.090	0.40	3.97[c]
24 Paraganas	1956-57	0.48	0.69	0.076	0.92	83.73[a]
Bombay						
Irrigated wheat Ahmednagar	1956-57	1.00	−0.28	0.120	0.46	5.43[c]
Dry Bajri Ahmednagar	1956-57	1.89	−0.30	0.074	0.72	16.28[a]
Nasik	1956-57	2.14	−0.41	0.109	0.69	14.15[a]
Dry gram Ahmednagar	1956-57	−0.01	0.33	0.170	0.39	3.82[c]
Irrigated gram Ahmednagar	1956-57	0.18	0.42	0.173	0.49	5.95[c]
Madras						
Paddy season I	1956-57	1.59	−0.17	0.04	0.70	15.30[a]
Paddy season II	1955-56	1.42	−0.10	0.05	0.45	4.85[c]
U.P.						
Wheat irrigated	1954-55	1.20	−0.07	0.03	0.36	4.02[c]
Sugarcane ratoon	1954-55	2.73	−0.23	0.06	0.69	13.51[a]
Wheat unirrigated	1954-55	0.98	−0.13	0.03	0.75	21.26[a]

Note: [a] denotes significance at 1 per cent level
[b] denotes significance at 5 per cent level
[c] denotes significance at 10 per cent level

Table B.III *Individual crops: relation between yield per acre and size of holding*

State	Positive R(not significant)	Negative R(not significant)
Punjab	Wheat irrigated 1954-55	Wheat gram irrigated 1954-55 and 1956-57
	Wheat gram unirrigated 1955-56	Wheat gram unirrigated 1954-55 and 1956-57
	Desi cotton 1955-56 and 1956-57	
West Bengal	Aman paddy (Hooghly) 1955-56 and 1956-57	Aman paddy (both districts) 1954-55, Aman Paddy (24 Paraganas) 1955-56
	Aus paddy (Hooghly) 1954-55 and (24 Paraganas) 1955-56	Aus paddy (24 Paraganas) 1955-56
	Jute (24 Paraganas) 1955-56 and (both districts) 1956-57	Jute (both districts, 1954-55, Hooghly 1954-55)
	Pulses (both districts) 1955-56 and 1956-57	Pulses (both districts) 1954-55
	Potato (Hooghly) 1956-57	Potato (Hooghly) 1954-55 and 1955-56
Bombay	Dry wheat (Nasik) 1955-56 1956-57	Rabi jowar (Ahmednagar) all years
		Irrigated jowar (Ahmednagar) all years
		Dry wheat (Ahmednagar) 1955-56 and 1956-57
	Irrigated wheat (both districts) 1955-56 and 1956-57	
	Dry gram (Ahmednagar) 1956-57	Dry gram (Nasik) 1956-57
	Irrigated gram (Nasik) 1956-57	Irrigated gram (Ahmednagar) 1956-57
Madras	Paddy season I 1954-55	Paddy season I 1956-57
	Paddy season II 1954-55	Paddy season II 1956-57
	Irrigated cholam 1955-56	Irrigated cholam 1954-55 and 1955-56
	Irrigated cotton 1956-57	Paddy season III 1956-57
U.P.	Sugarcane planted 1956-57	Sugarcane planted 1954-55, 1955-56
	Wheat irrigated 1954-55	Wheat irrigated 1955-56, 1956-57
	Sugarcane ratoon 1956-57	Sugarcane ratoon 1955-56
	Gram 1956-57	Wheat unirrigated all years
		Paddy 1955-56, 1956-57

2.   *Intensity of cropping and size of holding*

The following functional relation was fitted to study the relation between the intensity of cropping and size of holding:

$$\log I = \log a + \alpha \log X$$

where   I = intensity of cultivation

and   X = (average) size of holding

         a, α are constant terms

Table B. IV *Intensity of cropping and size of holding*

State/district	Year	Constant term	α	Standard error	R²	F
Punjab						
Amritsar	1954-55	2.22	−0.04	0.02	0.48	6.75[c]
Ferozepur	1954-55	2.13	−0.05	0.02	0.34	4.25
Amritsar	1955-56					
Ferozepur	1955-56					
Amritsar	1956-57	2.34	−0.07	0.03	0.36	5.34
Ferozepur	1956-57	2.82	−0.19	0.02	0.94	46.65[a]
West Bengal						
Hooghly	1954-55	0.03	−0.03	0.04	0.11	0.76
24 Paraganas	1954-55	0.04	−0.02	0.01	0.30	2.66
Hooghly	1955-56	0.05	−0.09	0.02	0.85	32.09[a]
24 Paraganas	1955-56	0.05	−0.07	0.02	0.64	10.82[b]
Hooghly	1956-57	0.09	−0.51	0.04	0.26	2.11
24 Paraganas	1956-57	0.04	−0.09	0.03	0.55	8.05[b]
Bombay						
Ahmednagar	1954-55	0.08	−0.04	0.01	0.49	6.05[b]
Nasik	1954-55	0.09	−0.03	0.01	0.38	8.35[b]
Ahmednagar	1955-56	0.03	−0.001	0.01	0.02	0.02
Nasik	1955-56	0.19	−0.10	0.02	0.70	14.54[a]
Ahmednagar	1956-57	0.10	−0.04	0.02	0.30	2.62
Nasik	1956-57	0.19	−0.14	0.02	0.83	30.33[a]
Madras	1954-55	2.07	−0.13	0.05	0.37	6.18[b]
	1955-56	0.19	−0.20	0.03	0.90	51.27[a]
	1956-57	0.20	−0.16	0.05	0.66	11.60[a]
U.P.	1954-55	0.23	−0.11	0.02	0.86	38.29[a]
	1955-56	0.18	−0.05	0.01	0.71	15.29[a]
	1956-57	0.21	−0.07	0.01	0.86	42.84[a]
M.P.	(Double cropping was negligible in M.P.)					

Note: [a] denotes significance at 1 per cent level
[b] denotes significance at 5 per cent level
[c] denotes significance at 10 per cent level

The results of the fit and tests carried out thereupon are presented in Table B. IV above for each state and year. As will be observed from Table B. IV, the intensity of cropping is inversely related to the size of holding but while in Madras and U.P. it is statistically significant, it is not so for Punjab and Bombay for all the years. Madhya Pradesh has very little double cropping.

3. *Fragments per acre and the size of holding*

The following relation between fragments per acre and the size of holding was fitted to the data and the results of the fit are presented in Table B. V:

$$\log F = \log a + \alpha \log X$$

where   F = fragments per acre
and   X = average size of holding; a, α are constants

It can be noticed that the number of fragments per acre invariably decreases with an increase in the size of holding.

Table B.V   *Fragments per acre and size of holding*

State/district	Year	Constant term	α	Standard error	R^2	F
Punjab						
	1954-57	0.50	−0.76	0.045	0.98	282.87[a]
West Bengal						
Hooghly	1954-57	0.64	−0.23	0.040	0.85	33.04[a]
24 Paraganas	1954-57	0.65	−0.50	0.079	0.86	38.72[a]
U.P.	1954-55	0.34	−0.37	0.074	0.79	25.19[a]
	1955-56	0.41	−0.40	0.065	0.85	37.88[a]
	1956-57	0.37	−0.30	0.041	0.90	51.90[a]
Bombay	1954-55	0.30	−0.64	0.102	0.88	39.42[a]
	1955-56	0.17	−0.60	0.065	0.94	92.96[a]
	1956-57	0.29	−0.62	0.088	0.94	49.59[a]
M.P.	1955-56	−0.10	−0.49	0.031	0.96	244.66[a]
	1956-57	−0.13	−0.48	0.015	0.98	977.92[a]

Note: [a] denotes significance at 1 per cent level

Appendix C

Labour use

1. *Relation between earners per acre and the size of holding*

In order to see whether there is any relation between the number of earners per acre and the average size of holding we fitted the following relation:

$$\log E = \log a + \alpha \log X$$

where   E = earners per acre

and   X = average size holding

       a, α are constant terms

The estimated parameters and the results of statistical tests are presented in Table C. I below.

It will be noticed that there is generally an inverse relation between earners per acre and the size of holding which is statistically significant in the majority of cases.

2. *Labour days per acre related to the average size of holding*

We fitted the following functional relation between labour days per acre and the average size of holding:

$$\log L = \log c + \alpha \log X$$

where   L = labour days per acre

and   X = average size of holding

       c, α are constants

The estimated parameters and the related statistics are presented in Table C. II for total crop production and in Table C. III for individual crops. The following crops were considered: irrigated wheat, irrigated wheat gram, unirrigated wheat gram, American cotton, *Desi* cotton in Punjab; *aman* paddy, *aus* paddy, jute, mesta, potato, pulses in West Bengal; *Rabi jowar*, irrigated *jowar*, dry wheat; dry *bajri*, dry gram, irrigated gram in Bombay; irrigated wheat, sugarcane planted, unirrigated wheat, paddy in U.P.; paddy season I, paddy season II, paddy season III, irrigated cholam and irrigated cotton in Madras.

Table C.I *Earners per acre related to the average size of holding*

State/district	Year	Constant term	α	Standard error	R²	F
Punjab						
Amritsar	1954-55	−1.13	−0.50	0.100	0.89	25.69[b]
Ferozepur	1954-55	−1.55	−0.28	0.109	0.69	6.48[c]
Amritsar	1955-56	−0.32	−0.30	0.030	0.98	110.87[a]
Ferozepur	1955-56	−0.03	−0.81	0.117	0.94	49.09[a]
Amritsar	1956-57	−0.43	−0.23	0.097	0.74	8.50[c]
Ferozepur	1956-57	0.16	−1.05	0.209	0.88	23.97[b]
West Bengal						
Hooghly	1954-55	0.39	−1.22	0.239	0.81	25.87[a]
24 Paraganas	1954-55	0.20	−0.65	0.186	0.67	12.35[b]
Hooghly	1955-56	0.21	−0.68	0.072	0.94	89.93[a]
24 Paraganas	1955-56	0.27	−0.72	0.051	0.98	200.89[a]
Hooghly	1956-57	0.23	−0.76	0.068	0.96	123.73[a]
24 Paraganas	1956-57	0.16	−0.62	0.060	0.94	106.18[a]
Bombay						
Ahmednagar	1954-55	0.33	−0.83	0.065	0.96	179.87[a]
Nasik	1954-55	0.27	−0.73	0.048	0.98	269.29[a]
Ahmednagar	1955-56	1.85	−0.68	0.328	0.41	4.34[c]
Nasik	1955-56	0.38	−0.94	0.062	0.98	231.40[a]
Ahmednagar	1956-57	0.26	−0.21	0.048	0.74	17.68[a]
Nasik	1956-57	0.73	−1.06	0.168	0.86	39.67[a]
Madras	1955-56	0.58	−1.06	0.06	0.98	322.04[a]
	1956-57	0.45	−0.87	0.04	0.98	520.91[a]
U.P.	1954-55	0.15	−0.79	0.054	0.98	214.76[a]
	1955-56	0.16	−0.79	0.062	0.96	162.65[a]
	1956-57	0.28	−0.83	0.077	0.94	115.36[a]
M.P.						
Akola	1955-56	0.45	−1.05	0.063	0.98	275.54[a]
Amraoti	1955-56	0.46	−1.04	0.189	0.82	30.50[a]
Region (both districts combined)	1956-57	−0.21	−0.43	0.236	0.18	3.35

Notes: [a] denotes significance at 1 per cent level
[b] denotes significance at 5 per cent level
[c] denotes significance at 10 per cent level

Table C.II indicates that labour days per acre spent on 'all crop production' are inversely related to the size of holding generally, and significantly so in most cases. Relating labour days per acre on individual crops we find that in only a few cases, given in Table C.III below, the relation turns out to be statistically significant and is inverse. With regard to the rest of the crops, except in a few cases[1], the correlation coefficient, although statistically not significant bears a negative sign.

[1] The few cases having a positive but not significant correlation coefficient were: *aman* paddy in Hooghly (1956-57); *aus* paddy in Hooghly (1954-55 and 1956-57); pulses and potato in Hooghly (1956-57); *desi* cotton in Punjab (1954-55); dry and irrigated wheat in both districts of Bombay (1956-57); dry gram in Nasik (1956-57) and irrigated gram in Ahmednagar (1956-57).

Table C.II   *Labour days per acre related to the size of holding: all crop production*

State/district	Year	Constant term	α	Standard error	R^2	F
Punjab	1954-55	1.45	−0.10	0.02	0.86	19.40[b]
	1955-56	1.47	−0.10	0.02	0.92	46.16[a]
	1956-57	1.47	−0.15	0.02	0.92	47.32[a]
West Bengal						
Hooghly	1954-55	2.16	−0.11	0.07	0.31	2.75
24 Paraganas	1954-55	1.37	−0.20	0.09	0.44	4.59[c]
Hooghly	1955-56	1.81	−1.13	0.04	0.61	9.62[b]
24 Paraganas	1955-56	1.77	−0.27	0.05	0.81	26.11[a]
Hooghly	1956-57	1.85	−0.04	0.06	0.05	0.29
24 Paraganas	1956-57	1.67	−0.08	0.05	0.31	2.72
Bombay						
Ahmednagar	1955-56	1.79	−0.36	0.09	0.72	16.59[a]
Nasik	1955-56	1.85	−0.36	0.07	0.69	29.92[a]
Ahmednagar	1956-57	1.82	−0.43	0.07	0.83	29.78[a]
Nasik	1956-57	1.89	−0.45	0.04	0.96	101.62[a]
Madras	1954-55	1.95	−0.40	0.125	0.64	10.36[b]
	1955-56	2.07	−0.52	0.10	0.81	27.12[a]
U.P.	1954-55	2.16	−0.49	0.05	0.94	99.62[a]
	1955-56	1.88	−0.18	0.04	0.77	20.93[a]
	1956-57	1.78	−0.01	0.07	0.002	0.02
M.P.						
Akola	1955-56	1.60	−0.22	0.05	0.79	23.74[a]
Amraoti	1955-56	1.51	−0.11	0.09	0.19	1.46
Akola	1956-57	1.15	0.03	0.07	0.02	0.16
Amraoti	1956-57	1.12	0.05	0.13	0.02	0.15

Note: [a] denotes significance at 1 per cent level
[b] denotes significance at 5 per cent level
[c] denotes significance at 10 per cent level

Table C.III *Labour days per acre related to the size of holding: individual crops*

State/crop/district	Year	Constant term	α	Standard error	R^2	F
Punjab						
Irrigated	1955-56	1.66	−0.30	0.10	0.79	11.42[b]
wheat gram	1956-57	1.38	−0.02	0.02	0.88	24.63[b]
West Bengal						
Aman paddy:						
24 Paraganas	1954-55	1.66	−0.30	0.06	0.81	28.74[a]
Aus paddy:						
24 Paraganas	1955-56	1.18	−0.25	0.03	0.88	53.16[a]
Jute: Hooghly	1955-56	2.06	−0.18	0.09	0.39	4.01[c]
24 Paraganas	1955-56	2.07	−0.26	0.06	0.77	21.85[a]
pulses:						
24 Paraganas	1954-55	1.76	−0.53	0.13	0.72	16.30[a]
pulses: Hooghly	1956-57	0.11	0.18	0.06	0.38	8.59[b]
Bombay						
Rabi *jowar*:						
Ahmednagar	1956-57	2.02	−0.98	0.47	0.41	4.31[c]
Irrigated *jowar*:						
Ahmednagar	1956-57	2.16	−0.61	0.21	0.56	8.14[b]
Irrigated wheat:						
Nasik	1956-57	1.44	0.19	0.08	0.45	5.02[c]
Dry *bajri*:						
Ahmednagar	1956-57	1.51	−0.30	0.06	0.81	26.64[a]
Dry *bajri*: Nasik	1956-57	1.63	−0.34	0.05	0.86	43.55[a]
Madras						
Paddy season II	1955-56	2.23	−0.35	0.15	0.49	6.00[b]
U.P.	1954-55	1.63	−0.24	0.05	0.77	22.32[a]

Note: [a] denotes significance at 1 per cent level
[b] denotes significance at 5 per cent level
[c] denotes significance at 10 per cent level

Appendix D

Labour productivity in relation to the size of holding

In order to see whether there is a consistent and systematic relation between yield per labour day and the average size of holding, we fitted the following functional relation:

$$\log 1 = \log c + \alpha \log X$$

where   1 = yield per labour day

and   X = average size of holding

Yield was defined as gross value of output for total crop production and as output in physical units for individual crops.

It will be noticed that for overall production the correlation coefficient had a positive sign in the majority of cases but was statistically significant only in a very few of them.

For individual crops, except for the few cases recorded in Table D.II below, the relation was more frequently positive but statistically not significant.[1]

---

[1] The few cases of negative but statistically not significant coefficients were: dry wheat (Ahmednagar, 1956–57), dry *bajri* (Nasik, 1956–57), dry gram (Nasik, 1956–57) in Bombay, irrigated wheat-gram (1954–55 and 1955–56), unirrigated wheat-gram (1954–55), American cotton (1955–56), *desi* cotton (1954–55) in Punjab; *aman* paddy (24 paraganas, 1955–56), *aus* paddy (Hooghly, 1954–55), jute (both districts, 1956–57), pulses (both districts, 1954–57), irrigated *cholam* (1955–56) in Madras; irrigated wheat (1955–56), sugarcane planted (1955–56) in U.P.

Table D.I *Labour productivity in relation to the size of holding*

State/district	Year	Constant term	α	Standard error	R^2	F
Punjab	1954–55	0.79	0.04	0.12	0.02	0.06
	1955–56	0.69	0.21	0.09	0.64	7.86[c]
	1956–57	0.76	0.02	0.05	0.45	2.50
West Bengal						
Hooghly	1954–55	0.32	−0.03	0.06	0.03	0.16
24 Paraganas	1954–55	0.32	−0.04	0.14	0.01	0.07
Hooghly	1955–56	0.22	0.13	0.04	0.65	11.90[b]
24 Paraganas	1955–56	0.39	0.10	0.06	0.32	2.88
Hooghly	1956–57	−0.43	0.01	0.10	0.002	0.02
24 Paraganas	1956–57	0.63	−0.02	0.10	0.01	0.05
Bombay						
Ahmednagar	1956–57	0.46	0.08	0.11	0.07	0.45
Nasik	1956–57	0.31	0.02	0.08	0.005	1.24
Madras	1954–55	0.29	0.01	0.22	0.004	0.004
	1955–56	0.42	0.14	0.18	0.09	0.67
	1956–57	0.65	0.11	0.13	0.09	0.71
U.P.	1954–55	0.29	0.35	0.04	0.96	75.41[a]
	1955–56	0.25	−0.07	0.04	0.52	3.24
	1956–57	0.54	0.06	0.07	0.10	0.64
M.P.	1955–56	0.51	0.04	0.07	0.06	0.37
	1956–57	0.69	0.01	0.07	0.02	0.01

Note: [a] denotes significance at 1 per cent level.
[b] denotes significance at 5 per cent level.
[c] denotes significance at 10 per cent level.

Table D.II *Yield per labour day related to the size of holding: individual crops*

State/crop/district	Year	Constant term	α	Standard error	R^2	F
Punjab						
Wheat irrigated	1954–55	−0.46	0.12	0.05	0.67	6.41[c]
	1955–56	0.25	0.21	0.08	0.81	14.05[b]
	1956–57	−0.65	0.29	0.09	0.74	9.26[c]
Irrigated wheat-gram	1956–57	−0.65	0.21	0.09	0.76	9.26[c]
American cotton	1956–57	−0.86	0.11	0.02	0.86	19.51[b]
Desi cotton	1955–56	−1.41	0.46	0.08	0.99	29.87[b]
West Bengal						
Aus paddy: 24 Paraganas	1955–56	−0.66	0.17	0.06	0.67	8.32[b]
Jute: Hooghly	1954–55	−0.97	0.20	0.01	0.43	4.64[c]
Jute: 24 Paraganas	1954–55	−0.93	0.20	0.07	0.56	8.03[b]
Pulses: 24 Paraganas	1954–55	1.76	−0.53	0.13	0.74	16.30[a]
Pulses: Hooghly	1955–56	−0.87	0.23	0.08	0.56	7.83[b]
Potato: Hooghly	1955–56	−0.87	0.23	0.08	0.56	7.83[b]
Bombay						
Rabi jowar: Ahmednagar	1956–57	0.33	0.28	0.10	0.54	7.64[b]
Irrigated *jowar*: Ahmednagar	1956–57	−1.55	0.87	0.42	0.42	4.39[c]
Dry wheat: Nasik	1956–57	−1.24	0.26	0.09	0.59	8.96[b]
Irrigated wheat: Nasik	1956–57	−0.45	−0.47	0.14	0.66	11.91[b]
Dry gram: Ahmednagar	1956–57	−1.08	0.37	0.19	0.38	3.89[c]
Irrigated gram: Ahmednagar	1956–57	−1.09	0.38	0.19	0.39	4.05[c]

Madras (none significant)

Table D.II (continued)

State/crop/district	Year	Constant term	α	Standard error	R^2	F
U.P.						
Sugarcane planted	1954–55	0.50	0.17	0.03	0.81	25.88[a]
Sugarcane ratoon	1954–55	1.28	−0.44	0.18	0.50	6.14[b]
Sugarcane ratoon	1956–57	3.40	−2.28	0.97	0.48	5.51[c]
Wheat unirrigated	1955–56	−1.66	0.81	0.33	0.49	6.05[b]
Gram	1956–57	−0.77	0.34	0.11	0.62	9.77[b]

Note: [a] denotes significance at 1 per cent level.
 [b] denotes significance at 5 per cent level.
 [c] denotes significance at 10 per cent level.

Appendix E

Labour use and size of holding

1.   In order to see whether the allocation of labour to crop production varied significantly with the size of holding we fitted the following functional relation:

$$\log W = \log a + \lambda \log X$$

where   W = percentage of labour days spent on crop production

and   X = average size of holding

a, λ are constants

The estimated parameters and related statistics appear in Table E.I below.

2.   A similar relation was fitted with the percentage of labour days spent on cattle maintenance as the dependent variable. The results of this exercise are presented in Table E.II below.

It can be noted from Tables E.I and E.II that, in general, while the percentage of labour days spent on crop production increases with the size of holding, that spent on cattle maintenance varies inversely with the size of holding. However, the relations are not statistically significant in all cases.

Table E.I *Percentage of labour days spent on crop production related to the size of holding*

State/district	Year	Constant term	λ	Standard error	R²	F
Punjab	1954–55	1.59	0.09	0.03	0.76	9.55[a]
	1955–56	1.51	0.11	0.02	0.96	64.05[a]
	1956–57	1.52	0.14	0.04	0.79	11.35[b]
West Bengal						
Hooghly	1954–55	1.12	0.17	0.13	0.22	1.74
24 Paraganas	1954–55	1.20	0.03	0.19	0.009	0.02[b]
Hooghly	1955–56	1.06	0.33	0.13	0.53	6.90[b]
24 Paraganas	1955–56	1.15	−0.14	0.28	0.36	0.24
Hooghly	1956–57	1.21	0.22	0.08	0.53	7.17[b]
24 Paraganas	1956–57	0.96	0.28	0.15	0.36	3.43
Bombay						
Ahmednagar	1955–56	1.69	0.09	0.06	0.24	1.93
Nasik	1955–56	1.94	−0.12	0.09	0.23	1.86
Ahmednagar	1956–57	1.19	0.36	0.06	0.85	32.25[a]
Nasik	1956–57	1.59	0.18	0.04	0.62	10.15[b]
U.P.	1954–55	1.85	0.04	0.01	0.81	24.67[a]
	1955–56	1.79	0.09	0.01	0.86	37.11[a]
	1956–57	1.79	1.15	0.01	0.96	126.41[a]
Madras	1955–56	1.59	0.11	0.03	0.71	14.87[a]
	1956–57	1.74	0.001	0.04	0.0001	0.0007
M.P.	1956–57	1.00	0.43	0.08	0.79	23.40[a]

Note: [a] denotes significance at 1 per cent level
[b] denotes significance at 5 per cent level
[c] denotes significance at 10 per cent level.

Table E.II *Percentage of labour days spent on cattle maintenance related to the size of holding*

State/district	Year	Constant term	λ	Standard error	R^2	F
Punjab	1954–55	1.65	−0.07	0.06	0.30	1.34
	1955–56	1.70	−0.10	0.02	0.45	26.26[b]
	1956–57	1.75	−0.10	0.04	0.67	6.57[c]
West Bengal						
Hooghly	1954–55	0.72	0.26	0.13	0.40	3.97[c]
24 Paraganas	1954–55	0.17	0.09	0.37	0.01	0.06
Hooghly	1955–56	0.65	−0.33	0.58	0.05	0.33
24 Paraganas	1955–56	−0.15	−0.54	0.44	0.20	1.52
Hooghly	1956–57	0.75	−0.68	0.42	0.30	2.61
24 Paraganas	1956–57	0.25	0.25	0.59	0.03	0.17
Bombay						
Ahmednagar	1955–56	1.88	0.30	0.18	0.09	2.68
Nasik	1955–56	0.87	0.50	0.25	0.38	3.88[c]
Ahmednagar	1956–57	1.59	−0.05	0.07	0.08	0.51
Nasik	1956–57	1.58	−0.03	0.12	0.08	0.51
Madras	1955–56	1.80	−0.11	0.03	0.67	12.70[c]
	1956–57	1.65	−0.001	0.05	0.0009	not significant
U.P.	1954–55	1.48	−0.12	0.03	0.79	22.45[a]
	1955–56	1.63	−0.31	0.08	0.71	15.50[a]
	1956–57	1.73	−0.48	0.07	0.88	45.34[a]
M.P.	1956–57	1.55	−0.06	0.18	0.02	0.10

Note: [a] denotes significance at 1 per cent level
[b] denotes significance at 5 per cent level
[c] denotes significance at 10 per cent level.

Appendix F

Use of bullock power and total inputs in relation to the size of holding

1.   We related bullock labour days per acre to the size of holding fitting the following relation:

$$\log B = \log a + \alpha \log X$$

where   B = bullock labour days per acre

and   X = the average size of holding

The estimated parameters and the relevant statistics for total crop production are given in Table F.I and for individual crops, wherever statistically significant, in Table F.II below.

In order to see whether there was any systematic substitution between bullock and human labour across size-groups of holdings, we related the ratio between bullock and human labour days to the size of holding by the following functional relation:

$$\log \left(\frac{B}{L}\right) = \log a + \alpha \log X$$

where $\dfrac{B}{L} = \dfrac{\text{bullock labour days}}{\text{human labour days}}$

and   X = average size of holding

We present the results, in relation to total crop activity, in Table F.III. We find that while the relation is generally negative (implying higher relative use of bullock labour on smaller holdings) it is not statistically significant in most cases.

3.   We related the total cost of inputs per acre to the size of holding by a similar log-linear relation and found that there was invariably an inverse relation which was also statistically significant in most cases (see Table F.IV).

Table F.I *Bullock labour days per acre in relation to the size of holding*

State/district	Year	Constant term	α	Standard error	R²	F
Punjab	1954-55	1.44	-0.16	0.02	0.88	50.51[a]
	1955-56	1.50	-0.12	0.04	0.76	9.86[c]
	1956-57	1.29	-0.20	0.03	0.77	10.09[b]
West Bengal						
Hooghly	1954-55	1.27	-0.03	0.04	0.08	0.50
24 Paraganas	1954-55	1.37	-0.20	0.09	0.44	4.59[c]
Hooghly	1955-56	1.20	-0.03	0.03	0.09	0.75
24 Paraganas	1955-56	1.23	-0.12	0.04	0.56	7.87[b]
Hooghly	1956-57	1.28	-0.01	0.08	0.0003	0.03
24 Paraganas	1956-57	1.22	-0.03	0.06	0.04	0.29
Bombay						
Ahmednagar	1955-56	2.10	-0.75	0.33	0.90	22.31[a]
Nasik	1955-56	1.78	-0.35	0.11	0.64	33.77[a]
Ahmednagar	1956-57	1.68	-0.32	0.08	0.79	5.17[c]
Nasik	1956-57	1.89	-0.41	0.07	0.85	10.49[b]
Madras	1955-56	1.89	-0.47	0.09	0.81	25.88[a]
	1956-57	2.14	-0.67	0.09	0.90	51.69[a]
U.P.	1955-56	0.33	-0.13	0.14	0.22	0.88
	1956-57	1.62	-0.12	0.03	0.86	19.24[b]
M.P.						
Akola	1956-57	1.20	-0.04	0.04	0.13	0.89
Amraoti	1956-57	1.06	-0.01	0.08	0.0002	0.02

Note: [a] denotes significance at 1 per cent level
[b] denotes significance at 5 per cent level
[c] denotes significance at 10 per cent level

Table F.II *Bullock labour days per acre related to the size of holding: individual crops*

State/crop/district	Year	Constant term	α	Standard error	R²	F
Punjab						
Wheat irrigated	1954-55	1.53	−0.08	0.03	0.70	7.76[c]
Irrigated wheat-gram	1954-55	1.25	0.05	0.01	0.84	15.88[b]
Desi cotton	1955-56	1.56	−0.30	0.09	0.79	10.92[b]
	1954-55	1.09	0.10	0.02	0.85	16.84[b]
Unirrigated wheat-gram	1955-56	1.52	−0.21	0.05	0.90	25.69[b]
	1956-57	1.37	−0.11	0.05	0.77	10.04[b]
West Bengal						
Aman paddy: 24 Paraganas	1954-55	1.26	−0.14	0.07	0.40	4.04[c]
Pulses: 24 Paraganas	1956-57	1.14	0.10	0.05	0.40	3.95[c]
Potato: Hooghly	1956-57	−1.26	0.19	0.08	0.46	5.33[c]
Bombay						
Rabi jowar: Ahmednagar	1956-57	0.28	−0.44	0.18	0.49	5.90[c]
Irrigated wheat: Ahmednagar	1956-57	1.48	0.19	0.05	0.72	15.45[a]
Irrigated wheat: Nasik	1956-57	1.48	0.20	0.05	0.70	14.79[a]
Dry *bajri*: Nasik	1956-57	1.48	−0.28	0.07	0.70	14.40[a]
Dry gram: Nasik	1956-57	0.68	0.36	0.09	0.72	16.01[a]
Irrigated gram: Ahmednagar	1956-57	1.81	−0.26	0.07	0.71	14.17[a]
Madras						
Irrigated cotton	1956-57	1.17	−0.22	0.11	0.40	3.91[c]
U.P.						
Unirrigated wheat	1954-55	2.10	−0.23	0.05	0.79	22.59[a]
	1955-56	1.37	−0.16	0.04	0.77	20.96[a]
Irrigated wheat	1954-55	2.16	−0.18	0.04	0.72	16.42[a]
	1956-57	1.34	−0.06	0.02	0.53	7.09[b]
Sugarcane	1954-55	2.23	−0.34	0.08	0.11	18.08[a]

Note: [a] denotes significance at 1 per cent level
[b] denotes significance at 5 per cent level
[c] denotes significance at 10 per cent level

Table F.III Ratio of bullock labour days to human labour days related to the size of holding: all crop production

State/district	Year	Constant term	α	Standard error	R^2	F
Punjab	1954-55	0.32	-0.30	0.03	0.16	81.96[a]
	1955-56	0.04	-0.02	0.04	0.58	4.17
	1956-57	0.16	-0.18	0.03	0.91	38.84[a]
West Bengal						
Hooghly	1954-55	-0.90	0.14	0.06	0.49	6.05[b]
24 Paraganas	1954-55	-0.72	-0.01	0.08	0.003	0.02
Hooghly	1955-56	-1.09	0.05	0.08	0.04	0.30
24 Paraganas	1955-56	0.77	0.06	0.04	0.27	2.23
Hooghly	1956-57	-0.80	-0.03	0.12	0.0006	0.05
24 Paraganas	1956-57	-0.60	-0.01	0.07	0.0003	0.02
Bombay						
Ahmednagar	1955-56	-0.14	-0.07	0.11	0.05	0.38
Nasik	1955-56	-0.15	-0.08	0.10	0.08	0.54
Ahmednagar	1956-57	-0.21	-0.08	0.09	0.11	0.73[a]
Nasik	1956-57	0.27	-0.34	0.08	0.79	22.19[a]
Madras	1954-55	0.10	-0.16	0.07	0.45	4.91[c]
	1955-56	0.10	-0.06	0.09	0.06	0.43
	1956-57	0.23	-0.12	0.05	0.46	5.25[c]
U.P.	1955-56	0.33	-0.13	0.14	0.23	0.88
	1956-57	1.62	-0.12	0.03	0.86	19.24[b]
M.P.	1955-56	-0.33	0.05	0.08	0.06	0.41
	1956-57	-0.16	-0.05	0.05	0.14	0.96

Note: [a] denotes significance at 1 per cent level
[b] denotes significance at 5 per cent level
[c] denotes significance at 10 per cent level

Table F.IV *Total inputs per acre related to the size of holding: all crop production*

State/district	Year	Constant term	α	Standard error	R^2	F
Punjab	1954-55	2.53	−0.35	0.24	0.40	2.03
	1955-56	2.43	−0.18	0.03	0.85	31.37[b]
	1956-57	2.57	−0.20	0.04	0.92	36.47[a]
West Bengal						
Hooghly	1954-55	2.49	−0.15	0.05	0.61	9.47[b]
24 Paraganas	1954-55	2.38	−0.32	0.04	0.90	56.99[a]
Hooghly	1955-56	2.26	−0.17	0.05	0.64	10.31[b]
24 Paraganas	1955-56	2.27	−0.18	0.05	0.60	9.54[c]
Hooghly	1956-57	2.49	−0.11	0.05	0.45	4.98[c]
24 Paraganas	1956-57	2.22	−0.01	0.04	0.02	0.11
Bombay						
Ahmednagar	1955-56	2.25	−0.36	0.14	0.52	6.46[b]
Nasik	1955-56	2.25	−0.36	0.09	0.72	15.69[a]
Ahmednagar	1956-57	2.34	−0.48	0.13	0.66	11.66[b]
Nasik	1956-57	2.49	−0.52	0.07	0.90	59.85[a]
Madras	1954-55	2.42	−0.41	0.12	0.66	11.48[b]
	1955-56	2.52	−0.50	0.04	0.96	134.81[a]
	1956-57	2.62	−0.49	0.06	0.90	61.29[a]
U.P.	1954-55	2.74	−0.41	0.04	0.98	102.61[a]
	1955-56	−1.24	1.21	0.25	0.88	23.62[a]
	1956-57	1.04	−0.05	0.02	0.72	7.93[b]
M.P.	1955-56	2.01	−0.07	0.02	0.59	8.66[b]
	1956-57	1.90	−0.08	0.03	0.58	8.08[b]

Note: [a] denotes significance at 1 per cent level
[b] denotes significance at 5 per cent level
[c] denotes significance at 10 per cent level

Appendix G

Effects of irrigation

1. Relating the percentage of the total cropped area irrigated to the average size of holding by the following relation, we found that it was inverse in all cases but statistically significant in only a few. (See Table G.I below.)

$$\log\ I = \log e + \beta \log X$$

where $I = $ percentage area irrigated

and $X = $ average size of holding

        e, β are constants

2. We studied graphically the relation between the percentage area irrigated and earners per acre and generally found a positive although not systematic relation between the two.

3. We also studied graphically the relation between intensity of cropping and percentage area irrigated. While there appeared to be a general tendency for intensity of cropping to increase with the percentage area irrigated, the tendency did not show up clearly or systematically, the observations being widely scattered.

4. In order to see whether irrigation influences the relation between output (and inputs) per acre and the size of holding we compared the results of the log-linear fits carried out separately on irrigated and unirrigated holdings in Punjab (see Table G.II). A similar exercise with respect to 'partially irrigated' and 'dry' holdings in Bombay did not give any consistent results possibly because the 'partially irrigated' holdings had very poor quality and low level irrigation. We have not reported here the results of the functional fits for Bombay.

5. In the report on Bombay for 1955–56, information on yield per acre, costs per acre, levels of tenancy and of irrigation was provided for individual holdings. Holdings are classified in five groups according to levels of irrigation: (0) wholly un-irrigated; (1) up to 25 per cent of area irrigated; (2) 25–50 per cent area irrigated; (3) 50–75 per cent area irrigated; and (4) above 75 per cent area irrigated. Holdings are also classified according to five 'levels' of tenancy: (A) purely owned; (B) holdings with up to 25 per cent area leased-in; (C) those with 25–50 per cent area leased-in; (D) those with 50–75 per cent area leased in; and (E) those with above 75 per cent area leased-in.

Table G.I *Percentage area irrigated related to the size of holding*

State/district	Year	Constant term	β	Standard error	R²	F
Punjab						
Amritsar	1954–55	1.99	−0.05	0.04	0.28	1.21
Ferozepur	1954–55	2.02	−0.11	0.08	0.40	2.06
Amritsar	1955–56	2.01	−0.02	0.02	0.86	20.62[b]
Ferozepur	1955–56	1.85	−0.01	0.08	0.03	0.08
Amritsar	1956–57	1.93	−0.02	0.02	0.10	0.35
Ferozepur	1956–57	1.96	−0.08	0.07	0.13	0.44
West Bengal						
Hooghly	1954–55	−1.01	−0.09	0.93	0.0009	0.008
24 Paraganas	1954–55	1.67	−0.67	0.12	0.83	32.45[a]
Hooghly	1955–56	1.08	−0.34	0.20	0.34	2.99
24 Paraganas	1955–56	−0.68	−0.40	1.04	0.02	0.15
Hooghly	1956–57	1.57	−0.85	0.16	0.81	27.83[a]
24 Paraganas	1956–57	0.04	−0.01	0.26	0.0004	0.004
Bombay						
Ahmednagar	1955–56	2.03	−0.60	0.14	0.74	17.35[a]
Nasik	1955–56	1.31	−0.43	0.21	0.41	4.26[c]
Ahmednagar	1956–57	1.77	−0.42	0.13	0.62	9.72[b]
Nasik	1956–57	1.75	−0.57	0.10	0.83	27.54[a]
U.P.	1954–55	1.91	−0.08	0.03	0.62	9.52[b]
	1955–56	1.95	−0.09	0.04	0.50	6.26[b]
	1956–57	1.98	−0.06	0.01	0.81	25.77[a]
Madras	1955–56	1.65	−0.32	0.09	0.68	13.55[a]
	1956–57	1.87	−0.54	0.12	0.75	19.51[a]

Note: [a] denotes significance at 1 per cent level.
  [b] denotes significance at 5 per cent level.
  [c] denotes significance at 10 per cent level.

In order to see whether there is any systematic relation between yield per acre and size of holding among holdings of comparable levels of irrigation and tenancy, we plotted yield per acre against size of holding for some of the combinations of level of tenancy and of irrigation. There were very few observations at higher levels of irrigation (see Table 6.III). Hence the scatters were plotted only for these combinations where there were more than about six observations. We found that except for (1, A), i.e. owned holdings irrigated up to 25 per cent of area in Nasik, and (0, A), unirrigated and wholly owned holdings in Ahmednagar, the scatters revealed no systematic relation at all. The scatter suggested a log linear functional fit in the case of (1, A) holdings in Nasik and a linear relation in the case of (0, A) holdings in Ahmednagar. The estimated relations were:

For (1, A) in Nasik

$$\log Y = 2.26 - 0.42 \log X \quad \text{with } r^2 = 0.38 \text{ (significant at 1 per cent level)}$$
$$n = 22$$
$$t = 0.12$$

For (0, A) in Ahmednagar

$$Y = 73.38 - 2.67 \, X \quad \text{with } r^2 = 0.27$$
$$n = 12$$
$$t = 1.41 \text{ (significant at 10 per cent level)}$$

Table G.II   *Comparison of irrigated and unirrigated holdings: Punjab*

A. In respect of output per acre related to size of holding

Year	Type of land	Constant term	α	Standard error	R^2	F
1954–55	Irrigated	2.30	−0.06	0.03	0.49	3.00
	Unirrigated	2.63	−0.58	0.12	0.79	23.78[a]
1955–56	Irrigated	2.28	−0.07	0.02	0.17	0.62
	Unirrigated	2.03	−0.17	0.07	0.72	7.57[c]
1956–57	Irrigated	2.50	−0.16	0.04	0.81	13.59[b]
	Unirrigated	2.45	−0.07	0.02	0.90	25.88[b]

B. In respect of input per acre related to the size of holding

Year	Type of land	Constant term	α	Standard error	R^2	F
1954–55	Irrigated	2.45	−0.16	0.02	0.96	79.04[a]
	Unirrigated	2.33	−0.30	0.02	0.98	153.73[a]
1955–56	Irrigated	2.44	−0.14	0.03	0.88	23.30[b]
	Unirrigated	2.17	−0.19	0.04	0.86	21.21[b]
1956–57	Irrigated	2.60	−0.25	0.04	0.88	29.89[b]
	Unirrigated	2.40	−0.35	0.04	0.90	15.98[b]

C. In respect of bullock labour days per acre related to the size of holding

Year	Type of land	Constant term	α	Standard error	R^2	F
1954–55	Irrigated	1.42	−0.12	0.03	0.88	22.54[b]
	Unirrigated	1.43	−0.26	0.03	0.98	98.80[a]
1955–56	Irrigated	1.42	−0.18	0.04	0.88	19.34[b]
	Unirrigated	1.05	−0.01	0.06	0.001	0.001
1956–57	Irrigated	1.29	−0.06	0.04	0.59	4.57
	Unirrigated	1.06	−0.14	0.39	0.36	0.11

Note: [a] denotes significance at 1 per cent level.
     [b] denotes significance at 5 per cent level.
     [c] denotes significance at 10 per cent level.

Appendix H

Relative technical efficiency of production methods

In the preceding discussions we have compared productivities of individual inputs on different size-holdings, e.g. yield per acre, yield per labour day etc. The use of productivity measures in terms of individual inputs taken in isolation, however, can be misleading in judging the overall performance of different production methods — each represented by a different input combination. A comparison in terms of some measure of revenue, such as profits or farm business income (i.e. gross revenue minus paid out costs) is equally inappropriate if market prices are not uniform for all, and additionally so if the choice of methods is influenced by factors other than market prices. Further complications arise if the objectives of production are not the same for all producers so that we may not presume that all are profit-maximizers. The presence of non-marketed or non-marketable inputs or outputs adds to these difficulties. Such situations do arise and have been referred to at various places in the text.

Here we shall use, in order to compare the *technical* performance of various size-classes of holdings, an empirical procedure developed by M.J. Farrell[1] which gives measures of *technical* efficiency with respect to multiple inputs. Technical efficiency is defined in terms of minimum input requirements for a given level of output. A *technically* efficient method is to be distinguished from a price-efficient method; the latter results from choosing, of the set of technically efficient methods, the one yielding the maximum profit at stipulated input and output prices. Thus price efficiency involves additional assumptions about the market and the price system while technical efficiency relates to the technological possibilities alone.

The method consists essentially in plotting observations of inputs per unit of output for each size holding in a space of the same dimensions as the number of inputs; then forming a convex closure of the set of points and taking the appropriate part of this convex closure as the estimate of the efficient technical frontier. The hypersurface defining the efficient frontier is derived by stipulating two conditions on its shape; it is convex to the origin and no linear facet that is a component part of it has a positive slope. To illustrate with respect to two inputs, we first plot the observations as a scatter diagram, the input coefficients forming the axes. The technical frontier is formed of facets such as PQ, QR, RS extended to both extremities by (0, 00) and (00, 0) so that all the observed points lie on or above the facets forming

---

1 See M.J. Farrell (1957) and M.J. Farrell and M. Fieldhouse (1962).

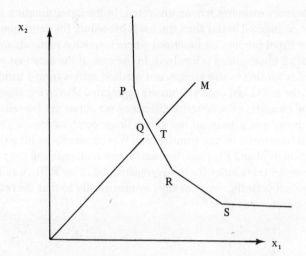

the components of the frontier and no facet has a positive slope. Algebraically, the points forming the facets are located as follows:

Let S be the set of n observed points (X_{ii}, X_{i2}); $i - 1, 2.......n$. If α_{ijm} and β_{ijm} are constants we solve:

$$\alpha_{ijm} X_{i1} + \beta_{ijm} X_{ji} = X_{m1} \qquad\qquad i \neq j \neq m$$

$$\alpha_{ijm} X_{i2} + \beta_{ijm} X_{j2} = X_{m2} \qquad\qquad i, j, m = 1, 2...n$$

for α_{ijm} and β_{ijm}. Then the line segment joining $S_i(X_{i1}, X_{i2})$ and $S_j(X_{ji}, X_{j2})$ is a part of the technical frontier if and only if $\alpha_{ijm} + \beta_{ijm} \geqslant 1$ for all $S_m(X_{m1}, X_{m2})$ in the set. Given the segments $S_i S_j s$ on the frontier, the technical efficiency of any point S_m can now be defined as the maximum of $1/(\alpha_{ijm} + \beta_{ijm})$ for all $S_i S_j$. The convexity of the frontier assumes that this is reached where $\alpha_{ijk}, \beta_{ijk} \geqslant 0$. Graphically the problem is to find the facet which is intersected internally by OS_m. In our diagram above, the efficiency of the observation M is measured by OM/OT which is less than or equal to one. This can be generalised in order to consider many inputs and outputs.[2]

The advantage of this procedure lies mainly in its ability to handle many inputs without raising the index number problem. An important shortcoming is that the measure of technical efficiency so derived will be very sensitive to any addition of new points or omission of existing ones if the points are such as to lie on the frontiers.[3] It is evident that if the omitted or added observations lie above the

---

2   See M.J. Farrell (1957).

3   A recent publication by Hati and Rudra (1973) develops a measure based on a continuous production function which does not have this shortcoming but which, as the method adopted here, uses the correct definition of the production function, namely as formed by points which give maximum output for given inputs.

frontier the efficiency measures remain unaltered. In the latter situation this method may be considered better than the usual procedure for derivation of iso-quants based on fitted production functions where regression methods are used and averaging of all observations is involved. In the case of the data that we use here, aggregated according to size groups, our method suffers from a handicap; to the extent that the individual observations are aggregated into size-groups, it is possible that the measures of productive efficiency we obtain are overestimated. To illustrate with the help of a diagram: not all the linear combinations of the points on the technical frontier lie on the frontier (e.g. W is an interior point although a linear combination of M and P). Thus, if observations on inputs and outputs are aggregated, the technical frontier for the aggregated data may shift away from the origin and, more importantly, may not shift symmetrically so that the *relative* rankings of efficiencies may alter.[4]

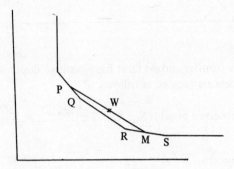

Further, in constructing the measures, the assumption of constant returns to scale is used implicitly in as much as the observations are in terms of inputs per unit of output. Ideally, if we have sufficient observations for each specified level of output, it is possible to work out the frontier for each such level and avoid this assumption.[5] The lack of such data necessitates relying on the constant returns to scale assumption.

We applied the method to derive measures of technical efficiency for different size-classes of holdings with regard to a few selected crops in selected regions. We considered four input coefficients: X_1, land per unit of output; X_2, human labour per unit of output; X_3, bullock labour per unit of output; X_4, seeds, manures and irrigation charges per unit of output. The maximum technical efficiency of an observation which lies on the efficiency frontier is taken as a hundred so that the relative efficiencies are all expressed in percentage terms. Although it is possible to present the efficiency frontier as built up sequentially by considering individual inputs successively, and then in all possible combinations until all the four inputs

---

4   See Bharadwaj K. and Bharadwaj R. (1965).

5   Also see M.J. Farrell and M. Fieldhouse (1962).

are considered simultaneously, we shall, for the sake of economy of space, give only the more interesting efficiency indices, namely, when land and labour are considered individually (i.e. for X_1 and X_2 respectively), for both land and labour (X_1 X_2) and for all the four inputs (X_1 X_2 X_3 X_4). Also we shall not present here the estimated coefficients for the linear facets, again in order to save space. We note from the empirical results given at the end that it is the middle size groups which show high measures of efficiency in a number of cases. For Punjab and U.P., when all the four inputs are simultaneously considered, the large holdings come up with high indices of efficiency (especially with regard to cash crops and irrigated crops). It may be recalled that these two regions have a better level of irrigation generally.

Although we have used the term 'technical efficiency', we should be careful not to attach any prescriptive or normative connotation to the term. It indicates only the outer-most boundary of the observed *technical* possibilities. However in our earlier discussions we have pointed out that input utilisation may be dictated by a number of considerations, e.g. inputs may be intensively utilised on small farms; as a result, inputs per unit of output may turn out to be high. Yet the small cultivator may find it desirable to employ such techniques although they do not lie on the technically efficient frontier and hence have less than a hundred per cent efficiency in this technical sense. The objectives of production as well as the availability of and accessibility of resources vary among the different cultivators. The objectives of production, in fact, are not independent of the resource position of the cultivator. (See Chapter 7.) In such a context the technically efficient frontier may not be interpreted as the set of feasible and *efficient* choices for all. In the context of competition, however, the technically efficient frontier does define such a set from which the set of relative prices picks out the price-efficient point.

Table H.I *Measures of technical efficiency according to size classes of holdings*

West Bengal

Crop, district, input	Size-group (acres) 0-1.25	1.25-2.50	2.50-3.75	3.75-5	5-7.50	7.50-10	10-15	15 and above
Aman Paddy								
Hooghly								
X_1	77	79	92	81	90	100	95	50
X_2	77	72	76	77	84	94	57	96
$X_1\,X_2\,X_3\,X_4$	81	77	82	82	85	100	64	88
$X_1\,X_2\,X_3\,X_4$	83	80	86	84	90	100	73	79
24 Paraganas								
X_1	81	71	79	67	86	77	25	—
X_2	57	73	86	75	93	100	43	—
$X_1\,X_2\,X_3\,X_4$	88	75	88	78	100	99	52	—
$X_1\,X_2\,X_3\,X_4$	72	80	92	80	80	100	38	—
Aus Paddy								
Hooghly								
X_1	58	83	67	59	100	86	62	—
X_2	30	100	34	24	44	55	41	—
$X_1\,X_2\,X_3\,X_4$	60	100	70	57	100	93	68	—
$X_1\,X_2\,X_3\,X_4$	60	100	70	57	100	93	68	—
24 Paraganas								
X_1	100	59	67	52	58	98	—	—
X_2	41	42	38	100	34	47	—	—
$X_1\,X_2\,X_3\,X_4$	100	76	77	100	67	100	—	—
$X_1\,X_2\,X_3\,X_4$	55	70	73	100	67	100	—	—

Table H.I (continued).
West Bengal (contd.)

Crop, district, input	Size-group (acres)	0-1.25	1.25-2.50	2.50-3.75	3.75-5	5-7.50	7.50-10	10-15	15 and above
Jute									
Hooghly									
X_1		63	66	100	63	70	48	66	—
X_2		53	51	39	76	100	68	70	—
$X_1\ X_2\ X_3\ X_4$		71	73	100	82	100	68	79	—
$X_1\ X_2\ X_3\ X_4$		75	77	100	79	90	62	81	—
24 Paraganas									
X_1		64	75	88	77	92	49	87	—
X_2		95	63	68	63	61	58	86	—
$X_1\ X_2\ X_3\ X_4$		93	85	98	87	100	63	100	—
$X_1\ X_2\ X_3\ X_4$		78	87	100	90	100	56	100	—
Pulses									
Hooghly									
X_1		96	59	48	67	63	61	61	—
X_2		100	60	64	88	80	76	77	—
$X_1\ X_2\ X_3\ X_4$		100	61	52	71	67	64	64	—
$X_1\ X_2\ X_3\ X_4$		100	61	51	70	66	63	64	—
24 Paraganas									
X_1		41	39	90	100	90	75	48	—
X_2		56	36	83	78	51	90	59	—
$X_1\ X_2\ X_3\ X_4$		44	40	92	100	85	79	50	—
$X_1\ X_2\ X_3\ X_4$		42	40	96	100	91	75	48	—

Table H.I (continued).
U.P.

Crop, district, input	Size-group (acres)	Below 5	5-10	10-15	15-20	20-30	30-40	40-50	50 and above
Sugarcane									
Meerut									
X_1		57	79	81	76		79	79	79
X_2		76	64	97	85		84	82	100
$X_1\ X_2$		75	82	100	90		91	90	100
$X_1\ X_2\ X_3\ X_4$		74	92	100	95		100	97	100
Muzaffarnagar									
X_1		80	95	90	96	95	100	89	93
X_2		65	76	69	69	88	67	66	71
$X_1\ X_2$		83	97	92	98	100	100	71	95
$X_1\ X_2\ X_3\ X_4$		79	93	86	90	100	94	91	88
Wheat Irrigated									
Meerut									
X_1		100	87	91	88	85	89	97	80
X_2		72	63	70	68	73	74	75	62
$X_1\ X_2$		100	87	94	91	92	95	98	83
$X_1\ X_2\ X_3\ X_4$		100	92	99	94	100	100	100	89
Muzaffarnagar									
X_1		80	82	72	84	80	93	78	75
X_2		75	68	56	65	100	70	67	54
$X_1\ X_2$		89	87	74	86	100	94	85	75
$X_1\ X_2\ X_3\ X_4$		91	93	78	91	100	96	90	78

Table H.I (continued).
Bombay

Crop, district, input	Size-group (acres) 0-5	5-10	10-15	15-20	20-25	25-30	30-50	50 and above
Bajri								
Ahmednagar								
X_1	100	93	64	64	43	39	35	21
X_2	42	51	48	47	45	104	53	40
$X_1 X_2$	100	97	71	70	52	54	51	34
$X_1 X_2 X_3 X_4$	100	100	84	82	63	68	73	51
Nasik								
X_1	89	82	75	64	71	71	46	54
X_2	79	86	90	70	97	100	70	83
$X_1 X_2 X_3$	100	100	97	79	99	100	67	78
$X_1 X_2 X_3 X_4$	100	100	97	79	99	100	67	78
Dry Wheat								
Ahmednagar								
X_1	46	58	37	47	27	38	38	39
X_2	56	80	61	74	47	84	80	100
$X_1 X_2 X_3$	57	81	61	75	47	84	80	100
$X_1 X_2 X_3 X_4$	77	100	61	81	55	96	93	100
Nasik								
X_1	47	86	62	100	76	60	95	100
X_2	52	59	55	84	61	53	98	88
$X_1 X_2 X_3$	53	86	62	100	76	60	100	100
$X_1 X_2 X_3 X_4$	65	90	79	100	78	61	100	100

Table H.I (continued).
Bombay (contd.)

Crop, district, input	Size-group (acres)	0-5	5-10	10-15	15-20	20-25	25-30	30-50	50 and above
Dry Gram									
Ahmednagar									
X_1		70	41	29	39	45	43	32	55
X_2		62	53	43	52	65	54	52	100
$X_1\,X_2\,X_3$		79	60	47	58	71	62	54	100
$X_1\,X_2\,X_3\,X_4$		100	67	46	65	78	71	55	100
Nasik									
X_1		59	62	61	49	54	42	57	100
X_2		35	46	42	36	39	39	39	75
$X_1\,X_2\,X_3$		49	61	57	48	52	69	54	100
$X_1\,X_2\,X_3\,X_4$		40	44	43	38	36	47	47	100
Irrigated gram									
Ahmednagar									
X_1		46	46	46	62	55	61	68	61
X_2		63	53	60	77	76	73	100	90
$X_1\,X_2\,X_3$		63	57	62	81	78	77	100	90
$X_1\,X_2\,X_3\,X_4$		55	52	57	71	71	76	100	100
Nasik									
X_1		62	93	96	100	41	17	77	67
X_2		53	45	82	88	47	22	91	63
$X_1\,X_2\,X_3$		61	56	93	100	50	23	97	70
$X_1\,X_2\,X_3\,X_4$		68	60	100	91	42	23	73	60

124

Table H.1 (continued).

Madras

Crop, district, input	0-2.5	2.5-5	5-7.5	7.5-10	10-15	15-20	20-25	25 and above
Paddy								
Coimbatore								
X_1	91	83	70	74	86	60	75	86
X_2	41	50	55	47	43	30	59	52
$X_1 X_2$	81	81	74	74	79	55	79	84
$X_1 X_2 X_3 X_4$	94	92	85	86	100	59	97	93
Salem								
X_1	100	72	70	82	64	91	—	63
X_2	65	59	47	63	44	85	—	100
$X_1 X_2$	100	76	71	86	65	100	—	100
$X_1 X_2 X_3 X_4$	100	91	81	100	73	100	—	100

Punjab

Crop, district, input	Below 5	5-10	10-15	15-20	20-30	30-50	50 and above
Wheat							
X_1	100	97	89	85	94	59	98
X_2	80	92	60	51	75	27	100
$X_1 X_2$	100	99	87	82	94	55	100
$X_1 X_2 X_3 X_4$	87	100	88	83	95	54	100
American Cotton							
X_1	93	100	63	89	79	53	100
X_2	57	74	64	62	84	84	100
$X_1 X_2$	93	100	63	84	79	53	100
$X_1 X_2 X_3 X_4$	85	100	85	91	100	100	100

References

Agarwala Ramgopal (1964a): 'Size of Holding and Productivity: A Comment' *The Economic Weekly*: April 11, 1964
– (1964b): 'Size of Holding and Productivity: Further Comments' *The Economic Weekly*; Nov. 21, 1964
Bardhan P.K. (1970) 'The Green Revolution and Agricultural Labourers', *Economic and Political Weekly*, Special number, July 1970
Bhaduri, A. (1973): 'A Study in Agricultural Backwardness under Semi-Feudalism', *Economic Journal*; March, 1973
Bhagwati, J. and Chakravarty, S: (1969): 'Contributions to Indian Economic Analysis: A Survey', *The American Economic Review*; Sept. 1969
Bharadwaj, R. and Bharadwaj, K.R. (1965): 'An Activity Analysis Approach to Measure Productive Efficiency in Agriculture: A Case Study of Ahmednagar and Nasik', *Indian Economic Journal*, Jan.–March 1965
Bhattacharya, N. and Saini, G.R. (1972): 'Farm Size and Productivity: A Fresh Look', *Economic and Political Weekly*, Vol. VII, June 24, 1972
Boserup, E. (1970): *Woman's Role in Economic Development* (George Allen and Unwin Ltd., London, 1970)
Buck, J.L. (1938): *Land Utilization in China*, University of Chicago Press, 1938
Chayanov, A.V.: *The Theory of Peasant Economy*, (Homewood, Illinois, 1966)
Chennareddy, V. (1962): 'Productive Efficiency in South Indian Agriculture', *Journal of Farm Economics*; Vol. 47, August 1965
Desai, M. and Mazumdar, D. (1970): 'A Test of the Hypothesis of Disguised Unemployment', *Economica* Feb. 1970
Dillon, J.L. and Anderson, J.R. (1962): 'Allocative Efficiency, Traditional Agriculture and Risk', *American Journal of Agricultural Economics*, Vol. 49, Nov. 1962
Farrell, M.J. (1957): 'The Measurement of Productive Efficiency', *Journal of Royal Statistical Society*, 1957
Farrell, M.J. and Fieldhouse, M.: (1962): 'Estimating Efficient Production Functions Under Increasing Returns to Scale', *The Journal of the Royal Statistical Society*, Series A , Vol. 125, 1962
Georgescu-Roegen, N. (1960): 'Economic Theory and Agrarian Reform', *Oxford Economic Papers*, Feb. 1960
Government of India; *Ministry of Food and Agriculture*: *Studies in the Economics of Farm Management for Bombay, Madhya Pradesh, Madras,*

Punjab, Uttar Pradesh and West Bengal; 1954–55, 1955–56 and 1956–57

Hanumantha Rao, C.H. (1963): 'Farm Size and Economies of Scale', *The Economic Weekly*; Dec. 1963

– (1965): *Agricultural Production Functions, Costs and Returns in India*, Bombay 1965

– (1966): 'Alternative Explanations of the Inverse Relationship Between Farm Size and Output per Acre in India', *The Indian Economic Review*; Oct. 1966, 1 (new series)

– (1968): 'Farm Size and Yield per Acre: A Comment' *The Economic and Political Weekly*; Sept. 14, 1968

Hati, A.K. and Rudra, A. (1973): 'Calculation of Efficiency Indices of Farmers: A Numerical Exercise', *Economic and Political Weekly*, Vol. VIII, March 1973

Hopper, W.D. (1965): 'Allocation Efficiency in 'Traditional Indian Agriculture', *Indian Journal of Agricultural Economics*, Oct. 1964

Khusro, A.M. (1964): 'Returns to Scale in Indian Agriculture' *Indian Journal of Agricultural Economics*, Oct.–Dec. 1964

Krishna, J. and Rao, M.S. (1965): 'Price Expectations and Acreage Response for Wheat in Uttar Pradesh', *Indian Journal of Agricultural Economics*; Jan.– March 1965

Krishna, R. (1963): 'Farm Supply Response in India – Pakistan: A Case Study of the Punjab Region', *Economic Journal*, Sept. 1963

– (1965): 'The Marketable Surplus Function for a Subsistence Crop: An Analysis with Indian Data', *The Economic Weekly*, Nov. 1965

Ladejinsky, W: 'Punjab's Green Revolution', *Economic and Political Weekly*, June 1969

Leibenstein, H. (1957): 'The Theory of Unemployment in Backward Economies', *Journal of Political Economy*; April 1957

Lenin, V.I.: *The Development of Capitalism in Russia*; Moscow, 1964

– 'The Agrarian Question', *Collected Works*; Vol. 5, Moscow 1964

Mazumdar, D. (1963): 'On the Economics of Relative Efficiency of Small Farmers', *The Economic Weekly*; Special No. July 1963

– (1965): 'Size of Farm and Productivity: A Problem of Peasant Agriculture', *Economica*, 1965

Mellor, J.M. (1963): 'The Use and Productivity of Farm Family Labour in Early Stages of Agricultural Development', *Journal of Farm Economics*, 1963

Mellor, J.M. and Stevens, R.D. (1965): 'The Average and Marginal Product of Farms in Underdeveloped Economies', *Journal of Farm Economics*, August 1965

Narain, D. (1965): *Impact of Price Movements on Areas Under Selected Crops in India 1900–1939*, Cambridge University Press, Cambridge, 1965

Paglin, M. (1965): 'Surplus Agricultural Labour and Development , Facts and Theories', *American Economic Review*, 1965

Raj, K.N. (1963): 'Investment in Livestock in Agrarian Economies' (Mimeographed 1968)

– (1970): 'Ownership and Distribution of Land', *Indian Economic Review*, April 1970

Rao, A.P. (1967): 'Size of Holdings and Productivity', *Economic and Political Weekly*; Nov. 1967

Rao, S.K. (1971): 'Interregional variations in Agricultural Growth 1952–53 to 1964–65: A Tentative Analysis in Relation to Irrigation', *Economic and Political Weekly*; July 3, 1971

Rudra, A. (1968a): 'Farm Size and Yield Per Acre', *Economic and Political Weekly*, July 1968, Special Number

– (1968b): 'More on Returns to Scale in Indian Agriculture', *Economic and Political Weekly*, Oct. 26, 1968, *Review of Agriculture*

– (1973): 'Allocative Efficiency of Indian Farmers; Some Methodological Doubts' *Economic and Political Weekly*, Jan. 20. 1973

Sahota, G.S. (1968): 'Efficiency of Resource Allocation in Indian Agriculture', *American Journal of Agricultural Economics*: Vol. 24, April–June 1968

Saini, G.R. (1968): 'Resource Use Efficiency in Agriculture', *Indian Journal of Agricultural Economics*, Vol. 24, April–June 1968

– (1969): 'Farm Size, Productivity and Returns to Scale', *Economic and Political Weekly*, June 29, 1969 *Review of Agriculture*

– (1971): 'Holding Size and Productivity and Some Related Aspects of Indian Agriculture', *Economic and Political Weekly*, June 26, 1971, *Review of Agriculture*

Sen, A.K. (1962): 'An Aspect of Indian Agriculture', *The Economic Weekly*, Annual No. Feb. 1962

– (1964a): 'Size of Holding and Productivity', *The Economic Weekly*; Annual No. Feb. 1964

– (1964b): 'Reply to Comment by Agarwala', *The Economic Weekly*; May 2, 1964

– (1966): 'Peasants and Duaism with or without Surplus Labour', *Journal of Political Economy*, Oct. 1966

Shrivastava Uma K. and Nagadevara V. (1972): 'On the Allocative Efficiency Under Risk in Transforming Traditional Agriculture', *Economic and Political Weekly*; Vol. VII, June 24, 1972

Srinivasan, T.N. (1973): 'Farm Size and Productivity: Implications of Choice Under Uncertainty; *Sankya*, Series B, 1973

Warriner, Doreen. (1939): *Economics of Peasant Farming*, London, 1939

Whitcombe, E. (1971): *Agrarian Conditions in Northern India*, Vol. I, University of California Press, 1971

Wise, J. and Yotopoulos P.A. (1968): 'A Test of the Hypothesis of Economic Rationality in a Less Developed Economy', *Journal of Agricultural Economics*, Vol. 50, 1968